June 1, 1944

Commander "Ace" Parker (sta[...]
as one-half of "A" Company boards boa[...]

Loading at the Port in England
for transport to the Ship taking
us to sea in the channel for the
invasion of normandie France

"I can't express how much I admire him. Just the whole package. He's definitely a memorable character."

Mary Walsh, CBS Producer

Reflections of Courage on D-Day
& the Days that Followed

"He was the kind of guy that nothing seemed to upset him. He had a cool head. Life was just a 'bowl of cherries'. An officer always used to carry a pistol but Ace always carried an M-1 and would cradle it in his arms like he was going out hunting deer or something. He reminded me of Davey Crockett."

John Perry
Private First Class
A Company, 5th Rangers

"I don't believe that there was a better officer than Ace Parker, and I would add to that, that all the fellas in the company I talked to felt the same way. He was fair, cool-headed and down-to-earth. He was dedicated, and he felt responsibility real strong. He cared about his men. He was just the kind of guy you followed. With a lanky stride, old Ace always carried that M-1."

Wilbur Ingalls
Staff Sergeant
A Company, 5th Rangers

Reflections
of
Courage
on
D-Day
& the Days
that Followed

A Personal Account of
Ranger "Ace" Parker

As told to
Marcia Moen & Margo Heinen

DeForest Press
Elk River · Minnesota · USA

Editor in Chief: Shane M. Groth
Cover & Book Design by Linda Thiltgen
Title Page Photos by David Ellis

REFLECTIONS OF COURAGE ON D-DAY
& THE DAYS THAT FOLLOWED:
A personal account of Ranger "Ace" Parker
Copyright © 1999 by Marcia Moen and Margo Heinen

Summary: The personal account of Charles "Ace" Parker, a World War II Ranger on the European Front, and his small part in the vast struggle against an intolerable threat to world wide peace and decency.

Requests for ordering books or for information should be addressed to DeForest Press, P.O. Box 154, Elk River, MN 55330. Phone (612) 441-9733.

Publisher's Cataloging-in-Publication
(Provided by Quality Books, Inc.)

Parker, Ace (Charles Henry), 1919-
    Reflections of courage on D-Day & the days that
followed : a personal account of Ranger "Ace"
Parker / as told to Marcia Moen and Margo Heinen.
— 1st ed.
p. cm.
Includes index.
LCCN: 99-75428
ISBN: 0-9649922-6-4

    1. Parker, Ace (Charles Henry), 1919- 2. World
War, 1939-1945—Campaigns—France—Normandy.
3. World War, 1939-1945—Personal Narratives,
American. 4. United States—Army—Commando
troops—History.   I. Moen, Marcia, 1954-
II. Heinen, Margo. III. Title.

D756.5.N6P37 1999   940.54'21442
                QBI99-1448

Richard DeForest Erickson, Publisher
Shane M. Groth, Editor in Chief
Linda Thiltgen, Cover and Book Design
David Ellis, Title page photos, p. 5

Visit our website @
www.deforestpress.com

Printed in Elk River, Minnesota, U.S.A. by The Total Printer

06 05 04 03 02 01 00 99   5 4 3 2 1

*This book is dedicated
to the
United States Army Rangers
of World War II
who gave their lives in service for their country.*

Ranger "Ace" Parker

Contrary to the beliefs of the uninformed, the Rangers were not made up of former convicts, super-athletes or general "tough guys". Men of the Rangers were average men, but with above average spirit, —every man a volunteer for an outfit that he knew would be assigned the more dangerous, more difficult, assignments of this war. For that reason, the "esprit de corps" of the Rangers had always far surpassed that of other organizations, and the spirit of cooperation and coordination was never absent from any assignment, no matter how difficult or seemingly impossible the task. This spirit was furthered by the leadership of the officers, the Battalion and Company Commanders, always in front of their attacking troops, setting an example for men who really needed no example.

–Henry S. Glassman
Lead the Way, Rangers, 1945

CONTENTS

FOREWORD

By Major Michael G. Zifcak (Retired)

In armed combat there are many perplexities, such as doubt, confusion, and bewilderment, to name a few. There also are variables and values involved requiring capabilities which must be applied to meet new, changing, and mysterious conditions and circumstances. Furthermore, those involved, and especially, but not limited to the leadership, are charged with certain necessities that can be learned from manuals studied and practiced. Manuals, however, must very frequently be tossed aside. Changing conditions may come into play dictating employment of on-the-spot decisions on a here-and-right-now basis.

Actions by the enemy in World War II usually required heavy support of firepower to accomplish our mission. Although this was written into our training, as per the sacred so-called "Fort Benning Solution," all too often that type of support for the Rangers was missing. Field expedience was required in lieu of the missing artillery, armor, engineer and air-rapid delivery support, much of which now is written into tactical and training plans.

Newness does involve confusion, lapses, misuse, and even disregard. This was very true with Ranger units in World War II, then new units in the Army Infantry alignment. Attaching them to larger units, particularly infantry divisions, meant that some of those commanders were not acquainted with proper deployment, utility of Ranger units, and proper allocation of adequate firepower for the Rangers. A glowing example was in the Saar-Moselle Triangle where the 94th Infantry Division Commander utilized all artillery support to his own division units and the 5th Rangers suffered the consequences at Oberleuken where small arms were our only means of firepower.

These failures became harsh reality and those who suffered most in leadership were the company commanders who faced the enemy in the "devil's workshop." In such circumstances, a unit can flourish in victory or fade in disgust. Fortunately, Company A flourished.

The reason for its success was that Company A had two of the most important ingredients any infantry unit must have for successful mission accomplishment. The first was that the company had an excellent leader, "Ace" Parker. The second was that the company had excellent followers. When an excellent leader has excellent followers, and vice versa, the chances for success are outstanding. There was mutual respect and support, so much so that the requirement for punitive action, with the exception of a few so-called "turkeys," was almost non-existent. "Ace" Parker had the qualifications of excellence, and the enlisted men were ever-ready to meet any challenge of any kind, regardless of unfavorable odds. In fact, odds actually were never considered.

In elaboration of Parker's leadership, one can mention his humanness to not only his men but the enemy. An incident exemplifying this occurred on D-Day when he and his men captured 13 enemy soldiers on the way to Pointe du Hoc. Quick judgment had to be made in either being burdened with the enemy soldiers or disarming them, freeing them, and reaching the Pointe where Parker and his men were desperately needed. He selected the second course of action and may have helped to open the later flood gates of Germans that surrendered in the northern sector of the European battlefield.

His winning the Distinguished Service Cross and later being inducted into the U. S. Army Ranger Hall of Fame were justified to the maximum degree.

PREFACE

"It was the adventure of a lifetime if you could live through it!"

So began one of many discussions we had with our uncle, Charles "Ace" Parker, as he reflected upon his experiences 55 years earlier in World War II. Ace is a World War II veteran and an Army Ranger who was among the first to cross the "bloody" Omaha Beach on D-Day, June 6, 1944. Charles Henry Parker, "Ace," was only 24 years old when the Second World War came to a crescendo on the day the combined Allied Forces stormed the coast of Normandy.

The 5th Ranger Battalion was in the second wave of boats to land that day. Ace Parker was a First Lieutenant at the time and Commander of A Company with the 5th Rangers. Ace's company, which numbered 72 men, were well trained and eager to make their mark in the war. He and 23 of his men were credited with moving further inland than any other Ranger group on D-Day.

On August 20, 1998, Charles Parker, along with 10 other Rangers, was recognized for his heroism and inducted into the Ranger Hall of Fame at Fort Benning, Georgia. It was this honor, along with seeing the movie *Saving Private Ryan* (released in 1998), that motivated us to ask Charles questions about his own experiences in World War II.

We listened, and soon his adventure became our adventure. Before this we knew little about our uncle's war experiences—only that he was a Ranger and had participated in the D-Day invasion. We regret we didn't know sooner.

Our interest led us to talk to Ace's men, who were also willing to share their memories. They spoke of Ace with genuine admiration. While time might have eroded the torments associated with their experiences of war, it had not eroded their gratitude for having served under their A

Company Commander, Ranger Ace Parker.

Saving Private Ryan opened our eyes to war, naked and real. The film left us stunned and shaken. We felt we had witnessed in a small way the reality of World War II and the Normandy invasion, and it scared us to death.

Michael Haskew, editor of the magazine *World War II*, described similar feelings when he saw the film: "War is ugly. War is waste. War is death. I left the theater completely exhausted and grateful that it was another generation that was obliged to take up arms and defeat the enemies of freedom. Every member of the armed forces who placed himself or herself in harm's way for our sake was and is a hero....Our veterans endured the harshest of conditions, forfeiting their youth, sometimes their health and too often their lives for their country. Acknowledging their sacrifice with a deeper understanding of their experience is the least we can do."(1)

This story is about Charles Parker and the men with whom he served on D-Day and the days that followed. Like many other men in World War II, Charles was a common man, raised by honest, hard-working parents, who was thrust into unreal circumstances by a world gone mad. It is the story of a hero. The men that served with him will never forget his unheralded bravery nor his sensible wisdom at a time when the world around them seemed utterly insensible.

War heroes don't live forever. Within a few short years, the stories may be lost in time. We encourage family members of war veterans to ask questions, to help trigger memories that might otherwise be forgotten. Honor them by listening to the memories. Write them down. Record them for others to read, so that we may always remember—freedom came with a price. The veterans of World War II know this only too well.

Marcia A. Moen
Margo A. Heinen

ACKNOWLEDGEMENTS

We would like to thank some special people that have contributed to the completion of this story about our uncle, Charles "Ace" Parker. First, we would like to thank our families for allowing us the long hours of preoccupation with this project. Randy, Marcia's husband, and our children, Alice, Joe, Heidi and Josh, all showed patience and encouragement. Thank you also to our parents, Leonard and Carmen Heinen, for instilling in us the belief that we could accomplish whatever we set our minds to do. We also wish to thank our sister, Christine, who unsparingly shared her special enthusiasm throughout the book's creation.

Thank you to Uncle Chuck's children, Jeff, Victoria, Laura and Katie for kindly expressing their gratefulness to us for putting their father's story on paper. We would like them to know that it was an honor and a pleasure!

Thanks to Uncle Chuck's living brothers and sisters for their support, interest and genuine encouragement: Muriel, Gerda, Glenn, and Carmen. Uncle Kenneth, now with us in spirit, always encouraged us to follow our dreams. Aunt Merle, Kenneth's wife, is greatly appreciated for the hard work spent in organizing all of Chuck's letters and photos.

Many friends and family contributed their perspectives and observations, books, and ideas that greatly contributed to the finished product. These valuable people were: Nicci Leingang, Tom Burdick, Kelly Clifford and Wayne and Christine Sticha.

A special thank you to Robert Askin (cartoon writer), son of Stan Askin (a platoon leader that served with our uncle and later became an accomplished writer), for taking the time to sift through his late father's writings. Thanks to him also for granting permission to publish Stan's story, which appears as a chapter in this book. Stan became a dear friend of Uncle Chuck following the war.

Thank you also to Mona Clark, daughter of Uncle Chuck's very best friend, George Miller (deceased). George was a fellow Ranger and company commander. Mona sent pictures and documents belonging to her father that contributed to the overall statement of this book. She also contributed much appreciated encouragement.

We want to extend our most sincere and heartfelt thanks to all of Uncle Chuck's fellow Rangers who were so giving of their time and memories. They showed us warmth and openness that exceeded our expectations. Their encouragement for our manuscript shall never be forgotten. We feel that we have known them forever.

Thank you, Michael G. Zifcak, for contributing the Foreword to our book. It was insightful in ways that we could never be.

We would also like to express our appreciation to our publisher, Richard Erickson, for his vision and for his willingness to put the whole project together under time constraints. Also thank you to our editor, Shane Groth, for his expert advice. Thank you, Linda Thiltgen, our art director. Her talent is real.

And finally, thank you to our uncle, Charles "Ace" Parker, who answered any and all of our questions untiringly. This is HIS story. Without his words and articulate way of capturing the memories, this book would not have been possible. He believed in us. For this we will always be grateful. He is our hero.

We hope you, the reader, enjoy the book.

THE RANGERS
AND WORLD WAR II

Rangers are an elite group of the Army Infantry—they are all *volunteers*! They have been used throughout America's history for special assignments in times of war. The Army Ranger exemplifies the highest standards of courage, initiative, determination, ruggedness, fighting ability and achievement. Rangers were the first American ground soldiers to see action against the Germans in occupied Europe during the Dieppe Raid.

American Army Rangers weren't activated at the beginning of the war. A couple of generals in Ireland decided that they wanted to have American units that were much like the Commandos of Canada and Britain. Churchill was also keen on the idea. This would create a unit much like the Rangers in early American history. They petitioned back to General Marshall in Washington, who was not only a brilliant military man but a brilliant diplomat. Marshall gave the go ahead. They decided on a leader. They picked one of their staff leaders who they greatly admired named Darby. Major William O. Darby organized and activated the 1st Ranger Battalion on 19 June, 1942 in North Ireland. This was the beginning of the Ranger involvement in World War II. The members were all hand-picked volunteers.

When the Army called for volunteers, the response was overwhelming, especially in light of the limited opportunities available. Soon thereafter the 1st, 3rd, and 4th Ranger Battalions were formed. These fought in Italy and North Africa. The 2nd Battalion was back in training here in this country. The 5th Battalion Rangers, the group of which Charles was a part, was the last to form as a unit and train.

The Fifth Ranger Infantry Battalion was activated on September 1, 1943, under provisions of an Army Ground

Forces letter, which included in part the following directive:

> All personnel will be chosen from volunteers of above normal mental and physical condition. Personnel should be under 28 years of age and should meet all physical requirements for that of a parachutist, excepting that he may not be required to jump from an airplane in flight.
>
> All personnel will be chosen from units which have completed and participated in a division-sized maneuver.
>
> Battalion will be prepared to undergo further directed training commencing January 1, 1944, as a part of an overseas command.

The history of the Rangers as a specialized fighting unit goes back to early America. In 1756 Major Robert Rogers recruited nine companies of American colonists to fight for the British during the French and Indian War. Unlike the wars fought in Europe that were based on recruiting men, training them, drilling them, and dressing them in bright uniforms and fighting "fairly," Rogers's Rangers used techniques characteristic of the American frontiersman. They fought the Indians as the Indians fought. They conducted themselves in the woods as if they were tracking and hunting a deer. This was the first time such a doctrine was used by a permanently organized fighting force.

The Rangers' involvement in World War II began with the Dieppe Raid on the northern coast of France along with the British and Canadian Commandos. Fifty Rangers participated and became the first Americans to die in the European theater. A lot was learned from that experience.

Ranger Creed

Recognizing that I volunteered as a Ranger, fully knowing the hazards of my chosen profession, I will always endeavor to uphold the prestige, honor and high "Esprit de Corps" of my Ranger Regiment.

Acknowledging the fact that a Ranger is a more elite soldier, who arrives at the cutting edge of battle by land, sea, or air, I accept the fact that as a Ranger my country expects me to move further, faster, and fight harder than any other soldier.

Never shall I fail my comrades. I will always keep myself mentally alert, physically strong, and morally straight and I will shoulder more than my share of the task, whatever it may be. One hundred percent and then some.

Gallantly will I show the world that I am a specially-selected and well-trained soldier. My courtesy to superior officers, my neatness of dress and care of equipment shall set the example for others to follow.

Energetically, I will meet the enemies of my country. I shall defeat them on the field of battle for I am better trained and will fight with all my might. Surrender is not a Ranger word. I will never leave a fallen comrade to fall into the hands of the enemy and under no circumstances will I ever embarrass my country.

Readily will I display the intestinal fortitude required to fight on to the Ranger objective and complete the mission, though I be the lone survivor.

Ranger's Standing Orders

The following Ranger's Standing Orders are carved in a large stone plaque that stands in front of the 75th Regiment Ranger Headquarters at Ft. Benning, Georgia. These orders were issued by Major Rogers in the 1700's during the Revolutionary War.

1. Don't forget nothing.
2. Have your musket clean as a whistle, hatchet scoured, sixty rounds powder and ball, and be ready to march at a minute's warning.
3. When you're on the march, act the way you would if you was sneaking up on a deer. See the enemy first.
4. Tell the truth about what you see and what you do. There is an army depending on us for correct information. You can lie all you please when you tell other folks about the Rangers, but don't never lie to a Ranger or officer.
5. Don't never take a chance you don't have to.
6. When we're on the march we march single file, far enough apart so one shot can't go through two men.
7. If we strike swamps, or soft ground, we march single file, far enough apart so one shot can't go through two men.
8. If we strike swamps, or soft ground, we spread out abreast, so it's hard to track us.
9. When we camp, half the party stays awake while the other half sleeps.
10. If we take prisoners, we keep 'em separate till we have had time to examine them, so they can't cook up a story between 'em.
11. Don't ever march home the same way. Take a different route so you won't be ambushed.
12. No matter whether we travel in big parties or little ones, each party has to keep a scout 20 yards ahead, 20 yards

on each flank, and 20 yards in the rear so the main body can't be surprised and wiped out.

13. Every night you'll be told where to meet if surrounded by a superior force.

14. Don't sit down to eat without posting sentries.

15. Don't sleep beyond dawn. Dawn's when the French and Indians attack.

16. Don't cross a river by a regular ford.

17. If somebody's trailing you, make a circle, come back onto your own tracks, and ambush the folks that aim to ambush you.

18. Don't stand up when the enemy's coming against you. Kneel down, lie down, hide behind a tree.

19. Let the enemy come till he's almost close enough to touch, then let him have it and jump out and finish him up with your hatchet.

Major Robert Rogers

"A" Company of the 5th Rangers landed on
the extreme left flank of the battalion. Even so,
"A" Company found itself intermingled with other units
on the beach. Lt. Ace (Charles) Parker set about
unscrambling the company and getting his squads and
platoons back into some semblance of order.
Reports showed "A" Company had virtually
no casualties crossing the beach.

For us in the second wave, still on the water and
less than five minutes behind, the noise had now
become deafening. An LCM or LCT to our right front
was hit by artillery fire and burst into flames.
Other artillery shell were detonating all around us,
with small arms adding to the inferno. The scene
was one from hell. Smoke from the fires on the
face of the bluff, fires from burning vessels
and equipment, black ugly puffs from artillery
bursting, dust and flying debris everywhere.

–John C. Raaen, Jr.
Sir, The 5th Rangers Have Landed Intact

Chapter One

D-Day, June 6, 1944

It was a slaughter.

—Ace Parker

WE WERE LOWERED down into the wild waters of the English Channel in our LCAs—Landing Craft Assault boats—about 10 or 12 miles away from Omaha Beach. The storm was raging. The waves were coming in so fiercely that the LCAs were going up and down, up and down like crazy. We were trying to push off from the mother ship using whatever we had in our hands that we could shove with. Anybody that was sitting along that side was trying to protect us as much as they could. If we hit the ship's side it would be a real jar and quite possibly could tip us, and, as I remember, some did. However, we didn't want to get away from the whole flotilla too soon either because the larger ships protected us a little bit from the wind.

The **navy** got the troops off about the same time so that the coxswains, the British seamen, could take us to where we were forming up, which was away from the mother ships. The British coxswains were experienced in Ranger landings. They had been there during the beach landings in Sicily, Italy and North Africa. When everything was in place and the leaders got the go ahead signal, we started in as a group. They didn't want there to be 30 minutes difference between when one boat hit the shore and when another one did. So, we gathered. We moved in a circle until Col. Max Schneider, the 5th Ranger

Battalion Commander and the only Ranger commander to have seen active combat previous to that day, gave the hand signal to form a single file and move in to shore. Every boat swung into a line parallel with the beach and moved in. When we were out there quite a ways, Pointe du Hoc, our mission objective, didn't appear that big. The background in the face of the cliffs made it hard to see. It became just another jagged piece of the coast line.

The storm raged on, and before we had gone very far we were bailing water. The water was coming in over the sides so fast that the pumps couldn't keep up with it. We were wet, shaking with chill and anticipation. The men spoke very little, sober but determined. The seasickness was so bad that vomit covered the bottoms of many of the boats—the men had used up all their vomit bags early on. By this time we didn't care whether we lived or died—bad seasickness will do that.

So now we went in. Machine gun fire, mortars, and 88 artillery shells were coming in all around us. The German 88 artillery gun was considered the best gun in the war, of either side. It could take down a plane, it was that powerful. The larger German mortars were effective and deadly as well, turning boats upside down and sending men flying up into the air. Whole boatloads were blown up before they even hit the beach. A couple of larger British boats were out there whose only assignment was to pick up men who had been thrown from the boat from enemy fire or tossed into the waters from the huge swells.

"Keep your head down! You'll see the beach when you get there!" Our boats were steel-clad. I was hunched down in front and I remember the sound of the bullets from small arms fire hitting the sides of the boat and bouncing off.

The flashing and smashing! Thousands of Allied ships of all descriptions were out there. There were rocket boats with their big banks of rockets firing like crazy. When they would fire all at once, it sounded like a screaming elephant. The battleships were out there throwing 1,000 pound shells in towards the beach, and they were exploding. To be honest, I don't think there was a lot of peripheral stuff that really impressed itself upon me. I was intent on getting to hell and gone—away from those big waves and getting into the beach and getting my feet on the ground.

It was quite awhile before we got in close enough to see what was happening on the beach. And when we did see what was going on there, we would just as soon try to put up with the water.

Some LCAs stopped in six feet of water or more, others stopped on a sand bar in ankle-deep water. Whatever was in front of them when they hit the beach, that's where they stopped. There were big ramps on the front of the boats, higher than the other sides, which were dropped down for unloading when we hit the beach. I could see other LCAs coming ashore along the beach to unload. The openings were crowded with men running off. The Germans targeted the openings and the minute the front end lowered they just mowed our men down with gun fire and some 88 shells for good measure. Many were blown up before they could even get off the boat. It was a slaughter!

Explosives were going off on the beach ahead of us—enormous sheets of fire from artillery guns, rifle fire and mortar fire. Machine gun fire was dimpling the water like it was raining here and there and was kicking the sand up on the beach everywhere. I remember seeing the tanks barely inching forward, unable to get a footing in the smooth, round rocks that lined the beach's shore. These rocks—shingle we called them—were flying out behind the tanks as they struggled to move forward. The tanks labored to get a bite in the sand before they could pull out and get away from the danger.

There were bodies laying all over the beach. There were bodies still alive in the water washing back and forth with the tide's waves. I could see Father Lacy trying to pull those bodies from the water onto the beach. We had no idea it was going to be this bad. Until you hit a beach like that, and this was the first one for us, you don't know a damn thing about what the situation is. It was far worse than we could have imagined. If anybody wasn't impressed about what was going on there, he'd be moronic.

I never had fear strong enough to rattle. I suppose a certain amount is fatalism. You've done what you can to be as good as you can. This is the condition you're supposed to be able to meet. So do it! Beat it!

We were lucky. The LCA I was in hit a sandbar, so the water was perhaps only knee-deep. When the ramp fell, our paralysis ended. Adrenaline lit the fires, energizing us into action. We moved ahead quickly onto the beach. We could see Pointe de Hoc only four or five miles down from us. The goal became to just live long enough to get off the beach.

We were never intended to do any fighting around the beach area. That was the job of the 29th Infantry who had landed before us. Our only assignment was to get off the beach and get to the Pointe. We had one thing on our minds—get to the sea wall and then check to see who else had made it.

The sea wall was a man-made wall, partly rocks and some wood, to protect the beach from erosion—from waves coming in. It was a long time before we hit the sea wall, even though we covered the distance at a dead run carrying all our equipment. We anticipated the resupply was going to be nonexistent until this thing was a success, so we were carrying everything we could. We had machine guns, individual rifles, mortars, and a few bangalores on us.

The rounded rocks of the shingle made it hard to run. It was as if we were in slow motion. We Rangers were in absolutely superb condition, but even we were slowed down in the final yards. We were slow-moving targets until we could throw ourselves down behind the sea wall and the meager protection it offered.

Everyone huddled up against the three foot wall. I was in

the middle of the group and one of the first to cross the beach. I looked down the line, two or three men deep, and saw shock, fear, bewilderment and excitement on my men's faces. This was our first stopping point. The first thing we had to do when we reached the wall was to gather the company and reorganize. I had all the men on me and got the company quickly grouped. The sergeants were counting. Though we had some casualties, we were basically intact.

A company is 65 men. But when we went in we were over strength by 15%, anticipating casualties. So we had 72 men. The report came back, "Company accounted for." I crawled to Max Schneider. "A Company here." We got the word to go and we knew what we needed to do. Time to move forward! We had learned in Ranger training to move, keep moving. If you stop you may die.

A wire fence lay before us. The barbed wire barrier lined the whole beach and prevented us from advancing. The wire was rolled wire, concertina type and barbed. It was taller than a man and of course staked down. The Germans had been there for four years and were well prepared for an invasion. The next thing that had to be done was to get a bangalore torpedo in the wire barrier to blow a hole through it. "Bangalores forward!"

Bangalores were long, tube-like torpedoes. We loaded each section of the bangalore with explosives three or four feet long and screwed it into the next section. We kept screwing them together and fed them into the fence. Then we huddled down and blew it. The blown hole was just big enough for one man to get through. It didn't matter who went first; whoever was there just went. We wanted to get through the hole in the wire and beyond it before those Germans could come alive again and take more casualties.

Right behind the barbed wire was the mine field and the bluff. The brush had burned off, and we could now see where the mines were located. It was a helluva steep bluff, not quite cliffs. The Germans were sitting on the top of the bluff in foxholes and trenches, firing upon us. Prior shelling from the Allies, as well as the shells from the ships in the early morning that day, had set fire to the brush on the bluffs. That created a lot of smoke which aided in hiding us from the Germans. We couldn't see the Germans, but they couldn't see us either.

Some of the things that happened on that day were not planned for. Some helped us and some hindered us. It was part of the training to take things as they were and adapt to them.

We climbed as fast as we could through the smoke and mine field. By the time we got to the top of the cliff we were weary again. I had the whole company up there at the beach road or the tarvia (tar) highway. My platoon leaders stepped up to report to me. I crossed the road, taking a few of them with me. Zelepsky, my 1st Platoon leader, and part of my Headquarters group, were with me. The rest of the men waited, back across the highway, out of sight, quiet and always conscious of avoiding being conspicuous.

We were at the corner of an open field. It was a farmer's small grain field, probably wheat. As I remember, the grain had already started to turn yellow and was fairly high. An E Company lieutenant, Woodford Moore, was standing there with us. Apparently his company had been scattered around on the way up. While we were standing there, German snipers at the end of the field in a group of trees started firing at us. We were about six or eight feet out into the field. The minute those bullets started coming in we went down. Moore was unlucky. I can see him now. His skull had been blown away and he was passed out. His brain was exposed on one side of his face down to his cheek.

When the rest of us hit the ground, my sniper, Tec 5 William Fox, didn't. He just squatted. That's when the bullet caught him in the shoulder. It appeared to be virtually nothing, just a little round hole with blue around the edges right up in the top of the shoulder. At the time we did not know it but the bullet that hit Fox had ranged on down across his body and severed his spine. The wound didn't look too bad, however, particularly when compared to that of Lieutenant Moore. I mistakenly thought Fox would be fine and that there would be no hope for Lt. Moore.

I was lying there flat and could feel the sniper's bullets going into my pack. Unlike the normal packs most men had with shoulder straps, I had one that buckled up the front and back. It was made of cloth and had all kinds of pockets. I had that thing stuffed with extra rations, enough D bars (high calorie bars) to go a month, dried food and extra ammunition. I knew I had to get out of that darn thing because it was making me a good target. However, I had to stay flat while doing this. So I worked my hands underneath me to undo the snaps to release it. I also needed to undo the belt that held it around my waist. Thoughts went through my head. One of them was that if I had been wearing just a regular pack, it would have been a lot easier to get out of.

As I was wiggling around trying to get this done, I was aware that I was calling attention to my location as the grain rippled with my every movement. Finally I got it off and left it there. The only thing I kept when I got out of that darn thing was my pistol. I didn't even have my holster since that was attached to the belt I had just left behind.

I saw a farmer's drainage ditch just a few yards away when I dove down to take cover. So, I decided to roll to the side quickly and get into the ditch. The ditch was about seven feet wide and three feet deep, and was used to keep the fields dry. Being a coastal region, the rainfall there was abundant at times. It was on the western side of the field and ran in the direction we were going.

The word was sent down the line to the rest of the company that we were now moving forward in the ditch. Everyone was to follow. There was only one way to go, however, and that was towards those snipers. Fox couldn't move, other than his upper body and arms. We crouched low and dragged him and Moore into the ditch out of harm's way. We provided minimal aid. Everybody had his own medical packet with sulfa (antibiotic), bandages and tape.

We gave a canteen of water to Fox and told him that others would be along to assist him when looking for casualties. We all had to crawl over Moore and Fox as we moved out. Fox waved and smiled. We found out later that Fox ended up dying in that ditch. Moore, however, was still alive when a rescue team found him. They shipped him back to England and then on to the United States. After much rehabilitation, he miraculously regained his speech, the function of his limbs, and later married and had a family.

We all kept down, crawling on all fours as the Germans were still working on us. We progressed along single file. We wanted to give the guy in front of us room to maneuver so we were spread out a little. Sometimes there would be two or three of the men bunched up together and then there might be a gap of 20 to 30 feet. We made very slow progress. What I didn't know, was that one of my platoon leaders, part way down the line, received a wound to his hand. Startled, he stood up and broke the continuity of the column. The rest of the group behind the wounded officer stayed behind and failed to move forward. They never crossed the road. This divided my company in two. Since I was at the head of the column in the ditch with my head down and crawling along on my belly, I didn't know any of this. I just assumed that everybody was following.

We were making very slow progress. No one was talking. We were using hand signals as we were in enemy territory. The rest of us got to the end of the ditch and took a sharp turn.

The German snipers that had been firing on us were located at this turn. We laid low and made it around the corner to the right. I found out later that several of my men, without my knowledge, took off into the woods at that spot to get the snipers. They never came back. They were either killed or most probably captured by the Germans. I would not have given the OK for such actions. That was not a part of our mission.

At this point we reached the barnyard of the Chateau de Vaumicel, our first rendezvous site. We advanced, leaving the ditch, moving carefully behind various objects in the yard, such as manure spreaders and small buildings. The barnyard had some wagons and some big draft horses. It was a working farm in an area of a lot of dairy farming. The chateau was considered by the locals as the "castle." Eight companies of Rangers were to rendezvous at this point, six companies of the 5th Battalion and two of the 2nd Battalion.

It was now about 2 o'clock in the afternoon. We had not eaten nor had anything to drink. We had other things on our minds. We came around to the front of the chateau. Stone fences enclosed the gardens. The owners appeared to be absent.

At this rendezvous point we were to meet, regroup, and then move forward. This would include counting men and so forth. So we counted. I was shocked. Only 23 of my men were still with me.

Charles & best friend,
Ben Hinckley

Parker family gathered near Rutland, North Dakota. Charles in front of mother on right

Chapter Two

Development of a Leader

My part as an infantry man will be a minor one. All that is merely my opinion—time alone will correct me or prove I'm right.

—Ace Parker

THE PLATOON UNDER my command was credited with moving further inland into the American sector than any other unit on D-Day. As the war raged on we were challenged by mission after mission covering the long journey across France and finally into Germany. Each day was a struggle to simply stay alive. I credit my survival to the training I received as an Army Ranger, which began several years earlier. Little did I know that the struggles and values I learned growing up during the Depression would prepare me for the greatest challenge to face me and my country.

I was born in Hecla, a small town situated in northeastern South Dakota, on May 13, 1919. My mother was a Swedish immigrant and my father was the local country doctor. My father, in fact, delivered me, just as he delivered all my brothers and sisters. (I was the third son and fifth child of six children.)

Living in America in the 1920's and 30's was not always easy. Often the doctor bills went unpaid by Dad's patients simply because the residents of Brown County did not have money during the Depression. They would pay instead with produce from the garden or home grown meat or other articles. I remember my father one day, tallying up the books. Fifty thousand dollars was on the books in money owed to him. At that point he made the comment, "If they don't pay me at the time of the house call, then they never will. So what's the use." He never kept any books after that.

Chores were a part of life at our house. My father believed that it was important to keep us children busy. Dad would acquire machinery from farmers. He would then instruct me and my brothers to tear them apart, recondition them and repaint them. Later, he would sell the machinery for a small profit. He also kept us busy moving wood piles. At one time, I remember, we had to tear down a garage and use the wood from it to build a shed. We then had to move the shed, once built, from one corner of our lot to another. This was all done to keep us busy and out of trouble, I'm sure. Not once did we dare to question his authority.

Another chore for us was digging multiple sewage disposals. The whole backyard was dug up at one time or another. Dad would have us dig a hole and a bunch of new trenches. We'd then lay the tile and divert the sewage from the sink. We didn't have an interior toilet, so the sink was the only thing that required a sewage disposal. We'd sink down like pocket gophers in the sandy soil. I remember standing in those holes and throwing the dirt over my head, they were that deep.

Requests to my father for money were often refused without explanation. I remember him saying 'No' to my petition for a dime. I had wanted to attend the movie uptown. I imagine he just didn't have the money. So, my brothers and I worked on farms or scrounged around town for odd jobs. We were known as hard workers, so we could usually find a job. My first time out thrashing wheat I made 15 cents an hour.

At age 17, the summer before my senior year of high school, my best friend and I dreamed up a plan to earn more money. Since times were so hard, my parents gave permission.

The harvest starts way down in Kansas and even Texas. The commercial harvesters would work their way forward up into the northern states of Minnesota, Wisconsin and the Dakotas.

Those states were always at the end because of how the climate affected the maturity of the crops. It was going to be a long time before the harvest was going to hit our area. So my best friend, Ben Hinckley and I decided that we'd like to hitch a ride down into southern Minnesota and pick up the harvest and work forward. Then we would get more time working the harvest and make more money. The money was needed for school, maybe to buy a new pair of shoes and jeans and also to have a little spending money. Ben and I did everything together.

My dad gave me three dollars to send me off. I was so impressed with the three dollars that I put the darn stuff down in my shoe. In fact, between my foot and my shoe. I didn't want anybody rolling me and getting that money.

We took off. We hitchhiked our first rides but pretty soon we were catching the freight trains. We generally cooked and slept out in the "jungle areas" where the bums were. That was an experience in itself. These areas were generally somewhere around the railroad tracks and stock yards. The stock yards were usually, in those days, around the railroads. That way they could load the cattle directly into the stock cars.

We quickly got clued in about how to ride the rails. Never, ever, ever catch a moving box car at its rear end. The rear end would be the back of the car from whichever direction it was going. You would want to be up at the front end of the car. When it was going at a fairly good clip we would run up there, grab at the front end of the car and the momentum would slam us against the side and hold us. Now we were aboard. But if we caught it at the end we would be flung back under the wheels. I've even ridden beneath the cars. We'd climb up underneath. There were all these bars and such. We would pick an area that would hold our body weight. The ground was right down there below us with the train going along at a good rate. There was plenty of clearance under there. If you were flat between the bars everything would pass under you.

However, we would be stuck there until that train came to a halt. Bums told us these little things.

They weren't all bums, you know. Relatively young men were riding the rails all over the whole countryside, trying to find a place for work. Jeez, you'd bump into anybody on those trains, like guys that were teachers trying to make some money during the summer. Railroad bulls or railroad cops had great empathy to people riding the rails. I don't know, maybe the railroads had an understanding of what the whole populace was going through. The railroad bulls would all carry a short club. They weren't as prevalent as they were later nor as strict as they became later on. Those guys became absolutely brutal. They would throw people off the train while it was going fairly fast.

We went to Laverne, Minnesota, right down in the corner of the state. They had been harvesting, but then the rains set in. We found out the carnival was in town. We hired out to them to put up the Ferris wheel. We had a devil of a time! First time they knocked the base out of plumb. That had to be perfect. So we put it up again. Soon, a cop came along and said that it was in the wrong place and on the wrong street. So we put it up yet again. All this was done for the original pay. Then the guy wanted to give us our money in tickets to the carnival. We had a good argument over that and we threatened to go to the police. We got our money out of it, however.

The harvest now moved north and we followed it. We returned home having supported ourselves for six weeks. I got back with exactly the three dollars that I had left with. Dad thought that I had done pretty darn good. I had supported myself. I'd fed myself. I hadn't spent any money.

I finished high school in June of 1937 and Ben and I began work for Roosevelt's work program, the Civilian Conservation Corps—CCC for short. I spent a total of one year with the project in the Black Hills of South Dakota. The first six months I labored as a stone mason and the latter six months at thinning timber. We also built a park headquarters. We were paid one dollar a day—which I worked hard to save and send home—and given food, shelter and clothing. Eventually the program ended because the armed forces needed men.

After the year was up, I returned home and learned that my father, in spite of hard times, had saved every penny of the money I had sent home. He had accumulated $300. It was enough to put me through my first year of school at Moorhead State College in 1938. Tuition was $18.50 a quarter and the remainder went for room and board. The next year I attended a small church affiliated college in Huron, South Dakota. The money had run out, but my older brother, Glenn, was able to help me get enrolled.

I had a job on campus for most of the tuition. I worked at Johnny Minolta's Greek Kitchen for meals and at a filling station and theater for cash. But I had no time for school and never claimed any credits from there. It was after that I got pulled into the army.

I was drafted into the army in 1941. I became a G.I., "Government Issue." The uniform, C-rations, and green socks were all government issue.

I felt a strong obligation to write home often as I knew my folks were wondering and worrying about me. I sent a letter from Huron, South Dakota, to let them know about the draft system.

March 21, 1941

In the past, from men I know who have been called and are in the army now, it's been about three months between their physical examination and the time they have to go. However, with spring and summer coming on and housing becoming easier, the quotas will be larger and selection much faster. Then, too, they have been getting only about three out of ten conscriptees.

```
The rest fail the second physical examination
at the main induction quotas. Volunteers are
falling off with summer work coming up and
that makes one's number come up faster. All
in all, I don't think it will be long before
I'm called for active service. My feet are as
flat as can be and may be deferred.
```

In June I announced the arrival of my draft letter. By the time I got the letter in the mail, there was so much news and hype about the war that pride allowed me to feel good about fighting for my country.

```
June 21, 1941

Well, Hello Everybody,
    I'm in the blooming army now. I've taken
the oath, had the articles of war read to
me, received my clothes and taken some
shots, one for small pox and one for
diphtheria. Just as fast as I'd bring up one
thing the doctors would discredit it. My
nose, they said, would be fixed (if it ever
bothered me), my feet weren't flat enough and
my leg wouldn't bother me. There was about
three hours of examination by around 15
medical examiners. Yessir, 15 of them. They
had a man for every nerve in the body.
    To top it off, a mental examiner
questioned us. He asked us about drunken
tendencies, insanity, nervous breakdowns,
nervousness, nervous disorders, epileptic
fits, venereal diseases and everything else
that might be inherent or acquired. He tested
our impulses and inquired about our social
views, whether or not we are friendly people.
He probed into our background, our hopes and
ambitions. In fact he knows an awful lot
about us right now.
    It's quite the game, this army life. The
food is excellent. The bunks not too hard
```

and the clothes have had some attempt at
being fit to the man. There is an old saying
though that goes like this: "The army fits
the man to the clothes, not the clothes to
the man."

You get a hundred orders a day, one of
which is necessary, the rest—disciplinary.
They march you a mile and a half, then when
you arrive at your destination it's only to
tell you to do something back where you
started from.

We don't get paid in this army until a
month after we get to our permanent station.
I don't know where that will be but I do know
that it won't be much before August 1st.

I'd have been in desperate straits if I
hadn't won a little money on the train en
route here. I had $1.15 which I knew couldn't
do me any good, so I "invested" it in a poker
game and won $6.00. That's gone now but I
have most everything I need.

No, don't worry—I'm not going to play
poker all the time. But I had to do something
or I wouldn't have been able to get along.
Now my address is:
Receiving Co. #2
Fort Snelling, Minnesota
And, oh yes, I'm Private Charles Parker.
All my love, Charles.

My first station was in Missouri. The coldest I've ever been
was at Fort Leonard Wood, Missouri, in the late fall. At that
time it was one of the most isolated camps in the whole
country. You had to have a weekend pass to go to town to get
a steak. It was way out there and raw—not even finished yet.
It would rain, rain, rain and that would become mud. It would
ball up on your shoes and each shoe would weigh about 15
pounds at least. Side walks! We spent a lot of time when we
first got there following trucks around and throwing rocks up

onto the flatbeds. We would truck the rocks back to camp to the Company and Battalion Headquarters and drop them into the mud. The glue would now become paths. So we would build a foundation by dropping those rocks on the paths between the barracks and on the paths to the company headquarters and around.

While stationed in Missouri I became a part of one of the greatest maneuvers ever held. Over a million men in this thing. We marched every day. We marched all the way down to the swamps of Louisiana. It was so early in the war that we carried a stick for a rifle. Different sticks were mortars. For tanks we used jeeps. The purpose of a big portion of this thing was just toughening us up. We marched all the way down from Fort Leonard Wood through Arkansas. That was all part of the tour. We put in something like twenty miles a day. It was summer. Everybody was still a civilian, soft. I remember the mosquitoes were relentless.

> Well, here we are on maneuvers. Right now we are at Fort Robinson, Little Rock, Arkansas. It's quite a life. Up at 4 o'clock everyday and sometimes at 3 in the morning. Then on night maneuvers we get up at midnight. The first day we rode on trucks. The 2nd day out we walked 22 miles. We walk only a half-day. The afternoon is spent resting, setting up tents, cleaning guns and equipment.
>
> On that 22-mile hike 700 men fell out. Three hundred passed out from heat and the rest from exhaustion or sore feet. I didn't fall out, but I don't know why or how I stayed on my feet. I think it was because another fellow in my platoon passed out. I don't like him and I wanted to beat him. I staggered and got dizzy, but I went on.
>
> Twenty miles isn't so far to walk alone. But marching in a company is extremely different. A mile in formation marching is

like 3 miles walking alone. It's the dust and pace setting, I guess.

The whole country where we maneuver is covered with a dense growth of oak trees. Here in Arkansas there is a profusion of different trees, but that is farther south. Everything is covered with a little bug called the "chigger." I am covered with chiggers. The bug is about half the size of a small pinhead. They can barely be seen by the naked eye, but their bite is worse than a mosquito. The itching the bite causes nearly drives you crazy. Wherever chiggers don't reach you, poison oak or poison ivy will.

Then they have numerous poisonous spiders and snakes down here. Everything that is needed to make life out of doors pleasant, including heavy rains. All of these are encountered while climbing steep hills through dense underbrush and carrying heavy guns.

All this isn't so hard to take, though. A man gets conditioned to go without sleep and to be on the run from dark in the morning through the day's heat to dark at night, through the night's cold. What gets one so confused and angry is the inefficiency and blundering. One day this week we went out on a "problem" and whole companies of men got lost. Another day we got up at 4 o'clock and lined out for a river crossing. A pontoon bridge had been erected and we were to cross on that. We got up at four and by 10 o'clock had just reached the river, even though we rode all the way (it was about 5 miles away). We sat around and waited. Four times we got on trucks and got off without moving or going any place. At 12 o'clock we rode down to the bridge—which was about 50 feet long—and we crossed and went home. While that was a very easy day, the waiting around made us so impatient that we were

all mad. There was no need to get us up at 4
o'clock in the morning. It's that sort of
thing that breaks the heart out of a man.
Certainly it builds no respect.

I haven't learned a thing. All the army
has accomplished with us men is to condition
us a little more. We are in better shape than
when we entered, but that end would have been
realized in a gymnasium much cheaper. Well,
"charge of quarters" just came through and
told us we have 5 minutes till lights out.
I'll write again after I've seen some more
country.

All my love, Charles.

I did not like snakes, but I had a squad leader that had a
phobia about snakes. I camped with him. We each carried this
shelter half or pup tent. So two men would have two halves
and that would make a tent. It happened that the guy that I
shared a tent with was Boyle, Corporal Boyle. He was also the
only man I ever met in my life to this day who didn't swallow,
that didn't have to swallow. Like when he drank water he'd
turn his head back, open up his mouth, take a canteen and pour
the whole canteen down his throat.

At night, the first thing we did was stretch out a mosquito
net on some poles and then we placed the canvas tent over it.
After that Boyle beat the ground almost to a pulp to create
impulses so the snakes would be gone. Then, we had to dig a
trench all the way around the tent because it was going to rain,
just sure as hell, at about four in the afternoon. It rained nearly
everyday. When the rain came down off the tent it would not
come underneath the tent. It would go into the ditch and run
off. But we also had to seal all the way around the bottom edge
of the tent with earth so no snakes could enter.

I've always had the kind of a bladder that prompted me to
go frequently. Even as a child. There in that tent I'd wake up
at least once, but generally a couple times a night, unzip first
the screen, then unzip the tent, but only part of the way. Then

I'd crawl out from under there. Of course, I was crawling across this wet ground now. So I was mud. I took care of my business and got back into the blasted tent. I zipped down everything, tightened it back again and patted the earth back in. I'll tell you, that going potty business took a considerable effort and time!

We returned to Fort Leonard Wood.

December, 1941
Fort Leonard Wood:

I should have written you when war was declared, just to allay any disquieting thoughts you might have had. However, I wanted to see the turn of events myself. Now I know that there is to be no great change in my army life for some time to come. What I mean is that I'll not be sent to any "hot spots" of the world. The new law permitting Congress or the President to send draftees any place in the world won't affect me for a while anyway. However, I'll be unable to come home for Christmas. I wanted to come this Christmas as never before, but it's impossible. Only 25% of the strength of the army can get furloughs at a time and only those who have never had a furlough before, get them. I will get a three day pass only because I've already had one furlough.

What I really wanted to tell you is that I'm fine. I feel fine and I'm getting along 100%. I don't want you to worry about me or the war. The U.S. will handle it and do so. I do think that it will be a long war because it's spread out so very much. My part as an infantry man will be a minor one. All that is merely my opinion—time alone will correct me or prove I'm right.

Charles.

December 1941

Here we are down in the orderly room,
griping, three of us from the north. We can't
have furloughs because we have already had
one. Even if we got a furlough it would be so
short a one that it wouldn't be worth the
trouble. By golly, aren't wars awful? Ha Ha!
Oh well, such is life—some build, others
tear down. There will be a lot of room for
the builders when the war burns itself out. I
plan on being one of these in some manner or
other.
I hope that the family doesn't get
excited about the war. It's here, we can't
change it, and I'm not going to get hurt.
I'll not even be exposed to danger for
sometime to come, if ever.
I'm a corporal now. We had mobilization
tests on progress and efficiency (within the
regiment) recently. I was the only one to
make a hundred on my weapon, which is the
mortar. That's out of nine companies.
Precision, speed, efficiency and
prescribed manner are all important. In order
to attain all of those capabilities, one must
drill and drill and drill. We've not been
able to do that yet.
Oh well, we'll get by. We're pretty darn
good—at anything. A bit of braggadocio, but
I've got to fool somebody! It's impossible to
fool these officers. You deliver—period.
I've talked about me. You talk about
yourselves and we'll know more about each
other.
Merry Christmas. All my love, "Chuck"

December 29,1941

Well, Christmas is over, has come and
gone. I know it has, for we got a day off and

had turkey dinner. Rumors fly thick and fast
in an army post. One man voices a thought and
60 others in one barracks hear him. Then
there are 60 men to repeat it. Within the
space of a few hours the whole camp hears. I
got so sick of hearing rumors on maneuvers
that I refused to let a man stay in my
vicinity if he repeated them. Now I ignore
them.

Here in the army the war caused a sudden
flurry, then we went back to regular routine
without a ripple of excitement. Men returning
from furlough tell of great excitement on the
outside over the war.

Officers warn of the seriousness of the
situation and advise us to train in earnest.
All expect to see action sometime and let it
go at that. I, for one, am glad it came to a
head so soon as long as it is inevitable. Now
army morale is much higher. We all feel that
we have a goal and a purpose for being here.
That was lacking before.

I'm not afraid, I'm a good soldier and
there is as much chance of dying of disease
on the outside as of getting killed in action
if you know your business. I plan to know my
business.

Write again, letters change a day to an
unbelievable degree. I don't get many 'cause
I write so seldom myself.

Well, take care. I'll be seeing you
sometime. All my love, "Chuck"

Down in Missouri, to get out of that blasted camp we'd
even volunteer to go to church. So, they would send us into
town to go to church, which was mostly Southern Baptist. (I
was raised Scandinavian Lutheran.) In the summertime there
would always be an outside picnic or a Sunday chicken fry at
one of the Baptist Churches. They always had those down
south and they always welcomed us. But we were obligated
to listen to the service. After church came the picnic with

southern-fried chicken, homemade ice cream, relishes, pies and the whole works. Good Lord the pies! They were the best.

In this one church, I can remember, there were probably a dozen of us in the church in uniform. The minister was a fireball and he was absolutely death on Roosevelt, our president. We were all thinking, "Well, he's our commander-in-chief." Not only that, but by this time I'm 21 or so, and that means I was old enough to have gone through the major part of the Depression when folks had nothing. Roosevelt came in to office. The banks were closing and everything else. He straightened all that out. He got the price of farm hogs back up again by killing all the excesses off. He had the pigs trucked out into the sand hills at home. A caterpillar built a big trench and the pigs were dumped down in there. The farmers stood on the sides and shot them. The same thing with calves and cows. Folks would say, "For Heaven's sake, there's so many people that don't have anything to eat. Why in the world didn't they at least give the poor people some of that meat?"

Roosevelt said, "Absolutely not!" What he was trying to do was create a shortage to create a market. Before this, there was no market; pennies per pound for a hog or a cow or a steer. So kill off the excess and now you've got a balance between supply and demand. The price comes up so a person can raise one of these things and make a little on it, pay for his work. People felt very, very strongly about Roosevelt. They either hated him or they loved him. I was on the side—well, I loved him.

So the pastor was up there berating against the war and would start raving about that "war monger" and "Eastern Jew" and that "ungodly Roosevelt." We would stand up in protest, be prepared to leave, even to start to march out. He would placate us, "C'mon fellas, c'mon now." He would get us set down again. In the meantime, we're thinking about that picnic. We'd blown it for any place else. We had to attend the church service to have a pretty good excuse to stay there at the picnic.

That was a different time! People would take you into their homes. They would come out to the camp and pick you up to go to dinner with them. I remember a bowling alley close to one of the camps. The fella that ran the bowling alley had a limousine. Every weekend he would send that limousine out to the camp and fill it full of soldiers. It would take a couple of trips. He brought us into Evansville, Indiana, so we could bowl for nothing and eat at the place for free. Then he would have us back on time! He did that every Sunday.

Then there were the communities that put up signs—"No dogs. No soldiers." They were against the war. They were against everything. But, generally speaking, those people down there were just absolutely magnificent. You had to work at making yourself unwelcome.

I remember a girl, as tall as I, a little bit gangly, and I called her "Em." It was during the summertime. The top would be down on her roadster and she'd pull up to the gate. I would meet her there and away we'd go to town. She was a buyer for a major newspaper. She would go out and scout the stores and check prices as a service to the patrons of the newspaper.

So I didn't have to go to town with a 2 1/2 ton truck with canvas over it. I got razzed, of course, by the guys. I think there was a certain amount of jealousy.

April 25, 1942

We are working harder than thunder and it's all day and all night it seems. I never had so many jobs and responsibilities when I was an enlisted man. Next Monday, the 26th of April, we go out in the field for ten days again. We've been practically living out there. Tomorrow I take my platoon out to fix a problem. It's a test by 3rd Corps Headquarters and it is pretty important. We fire live ammunition and high explosive shells.

In another three or four weeks I'll be a

1st Lieutenant if nothing happens. My
application has gone in to Washington
already. Now all I can do is wait until it
gets back.

Last Wednesday we marched 25 miles. Most
of the boys went to bed without eating
supper—they were so tired. A Sergeant and I
carried one man from my platoon in the last
3 miles. I felt fine, which surprised me a
good deal, but I'd forgotten how much
marching I've been doing the last 6 months.

Our training areas are 6 miles from the
company area so we get a 15 or 18 mile work
out every day. It has put my legs in good
shape. These men have been here for about 7
months and they don't get any sympathy from
me when they are tired. When I was in the
army 7 weeks we went on the world's largest
maneuver down in Louisiana. Remember? We
walked 125 miles in 5 consecutive days and I
was soft. We walked when we were tired and
dirty and hadn't eaten for a day or two or
three. You can get tired, that is REALLY
done in, when you've had a good night's sleep
on a bed and shower and a hot meal. Then you
only THINK you are tired. It's when you
haven't any core left inside that you are
tired. These men are in good shape. They've
had 7 months to get tough so they don't get
any sympathy from me.

I had my first brush with a ration book
of food today. I had to be down around the
quarter master commissary this morning so I
decided I'd get some food for lunching at
night. I went happily around the store
gathering sandwich spreads, canned meats,
pickles, olives, crackers and boxes of candy
in my arms. Then I carried them up to the
counter and wanted to pay for them. The
clerk said, "Have you got a ration book?"
"Ration book, what's that?" I asked. The
next thing you know I'm trotting around the
store putting things BACK on the shelves.

When I got through I had a box of crackers, a bottle of olives and one candy bar. There isn't much "lunch" value in that. All my love, Charles.

In May, I wrote home:

Monday, the 18th, I'm going to Fort Benning, Georgia, for officer's training. If I complete the three months' course I'll be a 2nd Lieutenant, a commissioned officer. I'm going to complete the course or it won't be my fault. It's very, very hard. They teach you in three months what ordinarily takes three years. The remainder of your education you learn while doing the job. As you can see the course is extremely intensive and many are dropped or failed before finishing.

Three months of drudgery, but I believe it's worth it. This is something that I can get my hands on and can apply and do in a practical way. We'll have about 65 books to study out of. Be good and take care of yourself and each other. All my love, Charles.

I made it through the officer's training. At that point, if you succeeded in passing the course, you were still considered just an enlisted man. So they had to discharge you from the army. You didn't even move. You reentered the army as a second lieutenant. Then came the assignment. That's when I got shipped out to Camp Breckinridge, Morganfield, Kentucky. I was sent to the 98th Division, which was an Infantry Training Division. I was a second lieutenant when I reported there and then I got assigned to a unit. One of the officers, "Stony," happened to know a college football player on the east coast with the name of Parker called "Ace." He was a very good football player and nationally famous. However, I'd never heard of him. (I had never heard of anyone or anything more than 100 miles from Hecla, South Dakota.) The first thing Stony did when he found out my name was Charles Parker, was to tag me with the name of "Ace." Of course the name went right along with me when I went into the Rangers. Some of the guys who had volunteered at the same time I did were also taken into the Rangers. So, they would call me "Ace." From then on I was Ace.

We had a regular gang. There were about four or five of us that were real close. We went together to raise the money to buy a car. We bought an old 1935 or 1936 Chevy of some kind. I think we only paid about $35 for it, but it ran. Gas back then was probably 15 cents a gallon. We broke a bottle of cheap champagne over the radiator cap and christened it "Private George." We'd park it, and when we went to get it on a weekend we might find that the gas had been all used up and nobody had replaced it. Guys would take it on their own— if we were tied up someplace and couldn't keep an eye on Private George. We had the keys, but as we found out, one really didn't need a key for it. They must have hot-wired it. That would've been at Camp Breckenridge. I think we parked it in the company area. We just left it sitting there when we transferred.

I was the alcohol officer for the Battalion Officer's Club. One of the barracks was made into an Officer's Club. I'd take a survey of who wanted what. It would be my duty to see that we didn't run out. Somebody else would be responsible for keeping the place clean and neat. Maybe we'd sponsor a dance and someone would arrange for music. Someone else would make sure that there would be girls there to dance with.

September, 1942
Camp Breckinridge, Kentucky

The people down in the country are

"Off-Duty"

wonderful, just as you said they would be,
Dad. We go to town and people stop us on the
street and ask us out to their homes for
dinner. They offer us their cars to drive.
And they try to get us to sleep in their
homes. We go to church and everybody in the
place insists on shaking hands. The minister
announces from the pulpit that there are
soldiers—officers—in the crowd and anybody
who has an extra piece of pie will please
take us home to dinner. Then 5 or 6 families
rush up and try to get us to come with them.

Hotels are building officers clubs
exclusively for officers. The people treat
the enlisted men nearly the same. They
organize clubs to entertain us when in town
and nobody tries to hold us up on prices
because we're soldiers.

September 7, 1942

Dear Folks,
I just listened to the President's talk
tonight. He was talking to an international
group of students. His speech was a beautiful
one, full of good sense and in Mr.
Roosevelt's usual beautiful cadence. When he
finished I turned the dial and got Mr.
Koltenbour, the news commentator. He told of
strikes and walkouts. Internal strife of all
kinds. I know that, that sort of thing and
those sorts of people are not what we men in
the army are fighting for. My personal
opinion is that we should take over those
plants and let the army stand guard.

We in the army take the brunt of the war
because we go out in the field against enemy
troops. We have only one mission and that's
to destroy or be destroyed. We lose out on
the chance to build a life of our own. We
miss the high wages or the chance to learn a
trade and a business. We even lose whatever

position we have gained in the world before the war. We are required to work hard and learn when the incentive to learn and work is taken away.

There is no inspiration of creation or salvation in the army. The driving force is the will to live, for we know that we have to be good to survive. Yet here we are, some of us are fighting on world fronts, the rest of us expect to be there sometime. I can imagine a soldier from the farm in North Dakota or a clerk from New York asking himself what he's doing in some jungle or desert thousands of miles from home, hunting to kill a man he's never seen nor who's never seen him.

There has to be a reason for it or men wouldn't, couldn't be driven to it. That reason must be home and family and the chance to live decently with family, dignity and freedom for ourselves. That's what we're here for, I guess. We read and hear about strikes in industry for better wages, shorter hours, and easier working conditions. That's fine. Perhaps it's necessary to employ violence to get a better way of life, but not now when we've already got the greatest struggle ever on our hands. When I hear some disgruntled, disgusted soldiers exclaim, "That's the people we're fighting for," I always think, No, it's not. We're fighting for our one chance at peace and happiness—and our people's chance at the same.

All my love, Charles.

October 20, 1942
Camp Breckinridge

Dearest Folks,
You haven't heard from me for some time, have you? Well, I'll try to make this letter

cover that lapse. To begin with, I'll
qualify my failure before I write any
further. There isn't any news. Everything is
the same from day to day. I'm enjoying a
break from Camp Monotony right now. I'm in
the hospital. Nothing serious—just skin
infections. It's in a rather delicate
place...a part of my anatomy which makes it
embarrassing as well as painful. I got a
skin rash from heat, sweat, and walking—in
the crotch. Then, having athlete's foot, I
spread that to the already worn and exposed
skin. That developed ringworm of a kind,
which spread rapidly due to sweat and wear
during marching. I went into the dispensary
where I received treatment for ringworm in
the form of a purple liquid. It seems that
the medicine cakes over, when applied
heavily and constantly for two weeks. Then
by golly, due to continued marching, the
cake cracked my skin and soon infection set
in. That's what I'm in the hospital for—
infection. It was pretty bad for awhile but
now it's nearly whipped.

Nurses! It seems like I'm always doing
something that I shouldn't. Like the other
night. I couldn't sleep when I first came
here. Hadn't slept for two nights and didn't
sleep the first two nights that I was here. I
just couldn't lie in bed from nine o'clock at
night until daylight, but that's what the
rules were. No lights!

About two o'clock I turned on the lights
and calmly began to read. Two minutes later
the night nurse, a Corporal of the guard, and
a ward-boy, all hit my door at the same time
and struggled for the privilege of turning
out both me and the lights. Some kind of
rule, I guess. Well, I subsided for the rest
of the night. Now I know there is a rule—no
lights after nine o'clock at night!

The next night I found that I couldn't
sleep again so about one o'clock I got up and

went into the toilet and the shower for my
room. I sat down on the floor of the shower
room to read. This, I thought, is my haven
from whence no nurse shall route me. Little
did I know about the metal of which the night
nurse is constructed, or I should not have
been so complacent! She looked in my room,
saw the empty bed and the light under the
door of the bathroom. Her thoughts
automatically followed a natural assumption.
A little later she looked again and found
that I was still gone. She wondered a little.
Still later she looked again. Same result.
Now she looked in the bathroom and I was
caught flatfooted. Reading!

Night nurse is a dirty-minded soul. She
saw her duty and did it. She took my pants! I
wasn't supposed to get out of bed, either.
That was two days ago and here I lie with
pajama top but no pants. Oh well, such are
the horrors of war. We have our tense little
moments every day when the sheets are
changed. I know these nurses are good at it
but they can't be infallible.

I bought a little flashlight through the
medium of one of the enlisted men working
here. At night when the lights go out at nine
o'clock I very slyly and cautiously pull the
blanket over my head, turn on the light and
read for about five minutes... just to show
my independence in defiance of the night
nurse. Of course no one knows it but me and a
few of the day nurses I've told, but it does
make me feel better. Now night nurse is
happy, I'm happy, and we do get on together
quite well.

Yesterday my door was closed and having no
bell to summon aid I lifted my voice in a
clarion call. I had no idea that it would
roar out so in the small confines of my room.
A colonel across the hall heard me, as did
everyone else. Thinking something was wrong,
he called out, and so did several others.

Result was that nurses converged from all
directions and were duly directed to my room.
They opened the door and I asked for a match
and a glass of water. My nurse (a cute
little redhead) and I are just now getting
back on smooth relations. Trouble is that she
is a second lieutenant...same as myself. Oh
well, that's the sort of thing that keeps
this place from getting humdrum. None of us
are very sick.

I'll be looking for a letter from you.
Until then, so long.

All my love, Charles.

April, 1943

Time has, and will, continue I imagine to
pass so fast that I have no conception of its
leaving me. These are times of great
activity for us, for time is growing short.
We are training these men for one thing, and
that is to fight on foreign soil. God
willing we'll never have to fight on our own
soil.

All my love, Charles

Dr. C. H. Parker
Lake Clinic
Bigstone city, So Dak.

SAINT PAUL
JUN 21
330 PM
1941
MINN

Hello Everybody,
Well here in the blooming army now. I've taken the oath, had the articles of war read to me, recieved my clothes and taken some shots, one for small pox and one for Diptheria.

Just as fast as I'd bring up one thing the doctors would discredit it. m.. nose, the..

minnesota, and oh yes, I'm Private Charles Parker address as so. You can write because they'll forward. All my love Charles.

Chapter Three

Join The Rangers

We never refused a mission and we never failed to accomplish one.

—Ace Parker

I WAS BORED, maybe because we never knew anything. Orders would filter down and we'd march half a day. We'd get there, we'd sit down and we'd never know what it was all about. We never heard anything about why we were doing what we were doing.

One day recruiters came through and put posters up on all the boards in all the barracks. "Join the Rangers!" "Join the paratroopers!" They were both recruiting. And I thought, The Rangers? Well, who were they? I immediately signed up for both. Whatever came along first, I felt, that's what I was going to join.

The Rangers got there first. It was a Monday. I remember it was on a Monday because I had been out on pass for the entire weekend and I hadn't slept. I had been partying like crazy. So, when I was inspected by the inspection board for the Rangers I was so fatigued that my heart was pounding really fast. After the examining doctor found out what I had been doing, he said, "Go over in that corner and sit down until your heart stops beating so fast." So I did. I came back up and he said, "Fine. We'll take you." The moment we joined the Rangers, as officers, we automatically became a First Lieutenant.

One of the reasons I decided to sign up for the Rangers was the caliber of the people that I was with in the infantry. The regular infantry in Kentucky had about a 15% limited service.

Limited service meant some had limited abilities. For instance, here's an infantry which most people expect to get around on their feet. One of the guys had a leg that was an inch and a half shorter than the other one. One of them was night blind. When we went out on night maneuvers it took a soldier on each side of the night blind soldier to get him through the blasted woods to keep him from falling down in the ditches and gullies. Large regular army units are confusing.

I also joined the Rangers because I realized that I desperately wanted to get into a unit that could influence events in battle situations. I preferred to be the "captain of my own ship." The Rangers were, and are, special mission troops. We were never used where ordinary infantry troops could do the job. We never refused a mission and we never failed to accomplish one.

I was shipped from Kentucky to Camp Forest in Tennessee for Ranger training. We were physically stretched to our limits and not all men passed. They were dropped.

I was very impressed with the men that trained us called the Cadre. They were the Rangers that had been in North Africa and Sicily. The training was ten times more intense than training with the infantry. It was here that the 5th Ranger Battalion was formed.

While we were down in Camp Forrest, it was initiated and reinforced that we take our rifles with us 24 hours a day—even to the movies. We would stack them teepee fashion out in the lobby. One corporal was assigned to stay there to guard the rifles. The idea was that we had to be able to respond instantly. This may not have always been the case, but it was for a length of time. It was another disciplinarian thing.

The M-1 rifle became such an integral part of every man's being that he would just aim and fire. It became a part of his body. He went to bed with it. Literally!

Our superiors invented strategies to teach us. I remember one particularly. We were given orders to rendezvous at a point across country and we were given a time to be there. They told us that they didn't care how we got there, we could take a taxi if we had the money, hitch a ride, but just be there. I can't remember if it was possible to get there by foot. But it was a "rat race."

Our last move was up to New Jersey. They gave us a few rations and immediately sent us out on maneuvers. We functioned as a platoon and not as a whole unit. We had to sleep out overnight in the snow. We were to move from there to here during a certain time frame. The thing was we had a limited amount of time to be at a given point which might be 30, 40, or 50 miles away. I suppose we had a couple of days to get there. They were trying to keep us busy and train us for the winter prior to shipping us over. We were in New Jersey for a couple of weeks.

Our commanders knew exactly where we were as we kept in constant communication as to our whereabouts. The supply truck would come by and just drop off rations. They would simply bring the stuff unprepared, not sandwiches or canned goods that we could eat readily. These were just supplies. I remember they gave my platoon a ham as a part of our rations. There was nothing that we could do with a damn ham! So, we traded it to one of the farmers. He gave us hard cider and a few groceries.

They also dropped off a 25 pound bag of sugar. Sheez! Did those people out in New Jersey want that sugar! Sugar was hard to get as it was rationed to the civilians. We went up to the farmhouse and explained the situation. "We've got about 25 pounds of sugar here. We don't know what to do with it— we can't drink that much coffee. Could you folks use it? We've got X number of men here. What do you have to trade for it? Do you have potatoes or something that we could cook?"

I also remember the cider! They made apple cider themselves from their own apple trees. It was kept in a big barrel out on the front porch. Now the cold comes. The watery content of the cider crystallizes and gets to be almost ice. It drops the alcohol out to the bottom of the brew because that doesn't freeze. All they would do, I suppose, was add some sugar to the stuff and let it ferment, and it would form alcohol. Now when we drew from that spigot down there, which is at the bottom, the alcohol content of that part of the cider just drops you down on your fanny. In the cold, a few sips of that....It was the only thing good I remember about the damn thing. Of course I always hated cold.

> Dearest Mother, Dad, and Carmen,
> You asked about the Rangers once. Well, there's not anything that I can tell you as it is not to be discussed. Except that we are the best soldiers in the world. Including the British Commandos whom we resemble.
> Out of the millions of men in the military service of the U.S., there aren't over about 3,000 Rangers all together. We're good and we're plenty tough.
> There is a $50 bond coming home every month from now on. Where I'm going I'll not need much money. I'm getting ready to take a little more active hand in this war.
> This letter has got with it a last will and testament. It's a requirement of the army that everyone fill it out and send it home. You keep it for me.
> I wouldn't want to be with any other outfit in the world than the one I'm in now. We're good and we know it. We get special training. I carry a sub machine gun myself, like a Chicago gangster did.
> I'm the next one in line for a company of my own. When there's a vacancy I'll get it, and then get to be captain.
> We all knew when we joined this outfit that it would be hard work, and it is. We

normally walk 5 miles an hour and quite
normally work all night until two or three in
the morning. Then a few hours rest and we are
at it again.

Just recently I worked 37 days in a row
including Sundays. I was in charge of one of
the committees to train the men on weapons.

Tomorrow I go out in the field and won't
be back until Sunday night. We move by night
and hideout by day. It will be a problem
trying to keep warm. If you carry enough
clothes and blankets to keep warm when you
sleep, you get too sweaty when you walk from
carrying the extra weight.

We have to walk. If you dress for marching
you freeze when you stop. I'll have to figure
out some sort of uniform and equipment to hit
both requirements. I have that responsibility
for my own men on this particular problem.
I've done it before so I guess I'll find the
answer to this one too.

The land is strange to me and I'll have to
follow maps to get my objective and
accomplish the missions. I don't worry about
it until I meet it, though.

UNITED STATES
OF AMERICA

War Ration Book One

WARNING

1 Punishments ranging as high as *Ten Years' Imprisonment or $10,000 Fine, or Both*, may be imposed under United States Statutes for violations thereof arising out of infractions of Rationing Orders and Regulations.

2 This book must not be transferred. It must be held and used only by or on behalf of the person to whom it has been issued, and anyone presenting it thereby represents to the Office of Price Administration, an agency of the United States Government, that it is being so held and so used. For any misuse of this book it may be taken from the holder by the Office of Price Administration.

the event of the departure from the United States of the per-
or her death, the book must be

No. 189032 .92

r the lawful holder
oid if detached con-
ardian may sign the
difficulties, or com-

lder

observed all the con-
Ration Book; that the
that an application for
ny behalf; and that the
st of my knowledge and

[Book Holder's
Own Name]

is or her own name

Mother

OPA Form N

to Certify that pursuant to the Rationing Orders and Regulations administered by the OFFICE OF PRICE ADMINISTRATION, an agency of the United States Government,

Certificate of Re

(Name, Address, and Description of person to whom the book is issued):

Parker (Last name)   Carmen (First name)   Patricia (Middle name)

Big Stone City (City or town)   Grant (County)   S.Dak. (State)

(Street No. or P. O. Box No.) _____ (Street or R. F. D.)

5 ft. (Heig

has been is
1942, upon
behalf by h

Local Board N

Stamps must not be detached except in the presence of the retailer, his employe

WAR & NAVY
DEPARTMENTS
V-MAIL SERVICE

OFFICIAL BUSINESS

U.S. POSTAL SERVICE NO. 1
MAY 2
12 - M
1944

Chapter Four

Ranger Training Overseas

Here I am in Jolly Old England.

—Ace Parker

AFTER NEW JERSEY we were shipped overseas. We hadn't gotten out of port when a freighter hit us. So we had to go back and repair it. The ship was towed back into the harbor for repairs. On January 8, 1944, we sailed out of New York harbor on the *H.M.S. Mauritania*, destination—SECRET. These were luxury ships that ran the ocean, like the Queen Elizabeth, only smaller. They stripped those ships to make them into troop carriers. After the war was over they would rebuild them with all the fancy staterooms and such. We were on our way the following day.

The "U" boats, or German submarines, were really slaughtering American shipping. The "wolf packs" that were out there sank hundreds and hundreds of thousands of tonnage of American ships carrying supplies. The ammunition that had been stock piled was going to be burned up in a whale of a hurry by a fighting army. So they have to have a set up to constantly replenish it. We're the only nation manufacturing on that scale and we're way over here separated by a whole ocean. The Germans knew that. That's where our ship convoys came in. They'd make up these great convoys. They'd all ship at once. They'd surround them with mine sweepers, sub chasers, and anything to protect them. But the "wolf packs" would lay out there and attack them underwater. Down would go the ships with the merchant seamen. The German subs were very effective. There were a few incidents with the troop ships, but the ships carrying troops were mostly much faster. So, it wasn't that we lost so many soldiers, but freight.

Of course, news of this affected us when we had to get on a ship to go overseas. But then we found out that Admiral Stark, who was the "he dog" of the whole Navy, was aboard our ship. So then we didn't worry. An escort plane would go out as far as its gas would allow—what the plane could carry—and then another plane would pick us up on the other side as soon as they could. But there was that space in between.

Our ship used a zigzag course for safety. We made a big "S" going over. I found out later that we went practically down to Bermuda. It took us 10 days. No storms. The wake of the ship going through the water would disturb the massive amount of organisms there. It was a delight to stand on the back of the ship and look at the phosphorescence, just a blaze of light in the water behind us. At nighttime it was just beautiful. I stood back there many nights.

February, 1944

Here I am in Jolly Old England. Had a fine trip over here and enjoyed it immensely. I've been here now for a little while so I'm somewhat accustomed to the monetary system and the customs of the country. The people here are wonderful and treat us very well. I'm in good shape except for sinus trouble, probably due to the damp weather. I'll get used to it. I'll keep you posted.

We spent our first months overseas at the commando training base in Achnacarry, Scotland, and on the cliffs of England and Wales. The Scotch were always known as very fierce fighters, and all the physical stress I've ever endured in my life was like a summer breeze compared to that month in Scotland.

I remember hitting the beaches in the cold clear Scottish waters. The Scotch commandos had a setup for training at Achnacarry. They would be on the shore, and if we didn't do it right we'd be out in the boats and do it all over again. We did an awful lot of boat landing, coming in on the beach, dropping off into that ice cold water of those damn Scottish fjords, getting sopping wet and then going on to the objective. We did this over and over again. We also did house-to-house-fighting training. This was in April.

On the 6th of May we moved to England, actually Wales. Here we worked on the cliffs, scaling and climbing ladders mounted on DUKS—amphibious vehicles that turned out to be not very helpful on D-Day. The ladders on these DUKS could be extended to 100 feet and had automatic weapons on top.

Once on top of the cliffs, we had to learn the right way to come down. Ropes attached to grapnel hooks were anchored in the ground a little way back from the cliff edge and swung over the edge to the beach. Squads and platoons lined up, and the leading man ran forward, leaned down, picked up the rope, pulled it across his body and continued over the edge of the cliff. When done properly, the rope held across our bodies diagonally held us back in against the face of the cliff—until we came to an overhang, of course. If we lost contact with our feet we would simply repel the rest of the way down. It was actually fun.

We had our allotments sent home. We kept just a little bit of the pay that we got for personal things, nights out and all that sort of thing. In Scotland at the commando training base we played an awful lot of poker and an awful lot of dice. I was hot!

Oh, jeez! Bob Stowe was our chief pigeon at poker. All you had to do was bluff him and then, by a little slyness, let him know what you had. He'd rise to take the bait. All you had to do was make it look like you were bluffing. If it was a good hand he'd come roaring in there. Very handsome fellow. We quite often took him with us to draw a few women when we went out.

We had men on detached duty down in England, preparing these places for us when we moved there from Scotland. Well, the pay day came when we were in Scotland. Everybody got paid, except the guys that were on detached duty down in England. Supplemental pay rolls for them, you know, and I was responsible for seeing that these men got paid. Well, several of the company commanders had that money and used it for playing poker. I won the entire troop's payroll from one of the company commanders. I put it in the bank, the Bank of England. At the time I had 400 English pounds, each pound worth somewhere between three and four dollars. Of course I loaned it back to him because he had to pay his men.

We billeted—housed—with a family from the area, but our meals were taken from our own cooks in the mess tent. There were some pretty strong friendships made between the Rangers and the British.

When we were in England, however, the British soldiers resented us being there. We had more money than the British soldiers—a lot more. And of course, the American soldiers were as aggressive as hell and the English girls were dating them. This was in addition to the normal rivalry that naturally occurs between two different groups. Then there was the rivalry of "who is the best at marching." Just the normal competitiveness. Sometimes it would boil over into fist fights. In their words, we were "over-paid, over-sexed, and over here."

The big hospital was there with all the nurses. It was during a slack time, so the nurses would throw a party or a dance and invite us. We'd all go. Then the USO would have dances and invite the English girls, and they would come. Brownie was a nurse with one of the field hospitals. Her last name was Brown, but I always called her Brownie. I can't remember what her first name is now. We became very good friends. In fact, that's all we ever were in spite of my very best efforts. She was short, kind of a round little girl, and a good dancer.

It was cold. England is always cold in the winter time. They don't know how to build central heating. And this was wartime, so fuel was in short supply. It was expected that if it got below freezing in the house...well, several times I was in bed with Brownie. But there was always a sheet between us. Not due to my efforts. Of course, when the invasion took place, I lost all sight of her. Her unit got sent to another hospital.

The captain of A Company was a spit and polish soldier. He was an old cavalry man, not an old man, but a cavalry man. Cavalry men are excessively proud. The cavalry always thought they were above that of the foot soldier. They ride the horses, you know, and had the long swords and all the spit and polish. The A Company captain went the whole bit of cavalry. He had a bat man. The bat man was considered to be the personal servant of the captain and would do things for the commander, such as shine his boots, and so on.

Things were additionally getting pretty tense up there at the commando base because we had no faith whatsoever in the Battalion Commander. All the company commanders were agitated about the Commander. The A Company Commander would have been among them because he liked to bitch about everything. He even, on a couple of occasions, assembled the company and marched them down to headquarters to complain about the medical treatment, something about "they had to wait too long." Yes, he was an agitator. Anyway, they called in the Inspector General to come down and see what the situation was with the whole unit. They agreed that the colonel needed to be removed from command of the battalion.

At the same time they decided to remove the A Company Commander. They took him out of the Rangers. This meant that A Company didn't have a company commander. So they looked at me and said, "We realize that you've been doing a good job as a lieutenant and we want you to take command of A Company." I was real happy.

When I was assigned a company in Scotland, the paperwork started for me to become a captain. The input for that would have been from the second in command, the executive officer, Major Sullivan.

I chose my runner along with other positions that needed to be filled. A runner is part of the headquarters group that you could use to carry messages. I could use my runner, for instance, if the radios were broken down. This happened frequently as those radios weren't all that darn good a half a century ago. They were big and bulky. Everyone knew that when the runner came with a message it was from the company commander. There was no arguing with him about where he got his information—it came straight from the commander. However, runners had a reputation for being the commander's bat man. Several lieutenants or captains utilized their runners that way, like servants. I picked the most troublesome man, McGuire, and told him he was going to be my runner. I knew he was going to kick and scream. But I told him, "You're not going to do a damn thing for me. I always do my own." I wanted him to be strictly the company's runner. I let him know that he would have the most dangerous job of all. While the rest of us would be hunkered down, he'd have to get up and move and deliver a message.

After our meeting, McGuire went and challenged the whole company, stating he had the most dangerous job as the company's runner. Would anyone like to challenge him for that position? He wanted the men to know he had a dangerous job. He turned his view and the company's view of the job around.

I had to put a stop to a little practice the fellows were pulling in England. In our training overseas we used live ammunition. As I came up one time on a group of my men, I could see them taking this practice a little too far. The guys would pull the pin on a hand grenade and let the handle flop up. You had three to four seconds after the pin was pulled before that grenade went off. The guy that pulled the pin would toss it to somebody else and he would toss it to a third person and he would then get rid of it. I came up there when they were doing this and they tossed it to me. I said, "That's enough of that!"

Being that close to a regular grenade, somebody was going to get their hand blown off, or worse. All I know is I wouldn't want to be on level ground trying to get away from a grenade when it blows—you're going to have 40 or so feet of explosive.

February, 1944

> The people of the United States don't know
> what war is, except that some man in his
> family isn't hanging around the kitchen
> anymore. These English folk do know,
> intimately, what war is and does. I never
> once fail to respect them for their courage
> and cheerfulness and generosity.

We weeded out a man from A Company before D-Day while we were still in England. We were behind wire in the locked up area as we were very close to being shipped over. They "sealed" us in so that we didn't have contact with civilians. They didn't want the guys shooting their mouths off in a bar and things like that.

This kid was on guard duty one night. The sergeant of the guard making his rounds had found him three quarters drunk and asleep while on duty. Something had to be done with him, and this was a court marshal offense. I knew that if we bumped it up, it would go through the whole army command thing and the kid would probably be thrown into a place like

Leavenworth for a real long long time. My other option was to give him company punishment. That means whatever I decide. So I gave him company punishment.

"Dig a hole six feet deep, like a grave, and bury the bottle." He couldn't do it during training hours, however. He had to do it on his own time. When he finally got the darn thing dug, I said, "Now throw the bottle down there." And he did. "Now fill the grave." So he did. As I was standing there I thought of another idea. I asked him, "Do you know which way the neck of that bottle is pointing?" Now any fool that is thinking at all would have said, "Sure, northwest..." or whatever. But no, he didn't know which way. So I said, "Dig it up again and let's see." So he dug it up again to see. Then we transferred him.

That was a lot better than a court marshal by higher headquarters. That would've been prison. He was a trouble maker and a wise guy. He had made a serious mistake drinking on duty. No self-discipline. So I chose to give him a company punishment and not a court marshal. That would have followed him the rest of his life. It was a big favor, whether he realized this or not.

It's considered that you are an elite soldier to be a Ranger. To fail to get into the Rangers in the first place is not a shame at all. But to have gotten in the Rangers and then to be kicked out would just make a man shudder. I saw a grown man cry when he was threatened with being kicked out of the Rangers if he didn't straighten out. He wasn't in my company. He straightened out.

I'm sure people wonder, when hearing this, why someone would he be so worried about getting kicked out of the Rangers, especially since they do some pretty dangerous things. It became pride that you could do your job as well as anybody else, and maybe better than most. Well, you felt that way as a Ranger. Pride wouldn't let you fail badly. There were some situations that you had to pull out of, but you did so in an orderly fashion.

Leadership depends on two things: pride and a sense of responsibility to the task, to the people, to the men you are responsible for. Also, the men have to believe that you're competent, that you know what you're doing, that if there is a way to win in a situation you're probably going to find it.

It's the same with the men. Their pride would not let them fail the squad or the platoon. Every man is responsible for every other man in a situation like this. Our people all knew each other. There was no situation where a sergeant did not know what a guy's name was because he hadn't gotten him down on the roster yet, for instance, as with a replacement. That happened an awful lot in the larger regular Army units. Replacements would come in, sometimes in the middle of the night. They'd shuttle him up to the front line, drop him off to a sergeant and say, "Here's your replacement, Sarge." He'd try to get their names written down on a piece of paper, but it didn't always happen. The battle would be joined. Some of these guys would be killed right away and they didn't even know their name. There was none of that in the Rangers. That was another reason that I got out of the regular Army.

"A" Company officers reviewing headlines of Stars & Stripes Newspaper. From left to right: Stan Askin, Stan Zelepsky, Cpt. C. "Ace" Parker, O. Art Suchier

Chapter Five

Our Country Prepares For War

I'm not afraid. I'm a good soldier and there is as much chance of dying of disease on the outside as of getting killed in action if you know your business. I plan to know my business.

—Ace Parker

GERMANY WAS DEFEATED in World War I by the Allies. According to the treaty, Germany was to be denied any manufacturing. It was to be turned into strictly an agrarian state. The only thing Germany was going to be able to do was to raise crops. Their money was worthless. Literally. You could take a wheelbarrow full of their money just to buy a loaf of bread. They were still in that situation when Hitler first started to form his group in a beer cellar in Munich.

Germany attacked Poland at dawn on September 1, 1939. They picked out a Jew and shot him. They dressed him in a polish outfit. They put him in there and made it look like the Polish had done it. That gave them the excuse to jump the border and attack Poland. Then Hitler went through Europe. He overran countries without getting anybody killed. His own troops didn't have to fight very hard.

On December 7, 1941, the Japanese attacked Hawaii. On December 11, Hitler declared war on the United States. Suddenly, the conflict was worldwide in scope. England was getting very weary and was on its last leg when America finally got really "tooled up". It took an awful lot of persuasion on Roosevelt's part before we really "bellied up to the bar" and built a war machine. But the Japanese bombing

Pearl Harbor allowed Roosevelt to rally the country and go all out for a war. He'd been working like crazy building the industrial area up to supply a war.

Lord a mighty, for a civilian to get a tire living in those years was really a miracle. All the rubber we had was devoted to the war. Food, of course, was also rationed using food stamps.

With America in the war in both Europe and the Pacific, new and enormous might came into play. We'd drive through the English countryside before the invasion and we couldn't believe what we saw! Tanks! Mile after mile of tanks sitting there. All American-made.

Churchill commended the British Air Force, "Never has so much been owed by so many to so few." He was talking about the English fighter pilot's success in destroying the German fighter planes over the Channel. They met as far out as they could and shot them down. And they got shot by the hundreds themselves. When they lost a pilot, they lost a plane. When they lost a plane, they lost a pilot. It was difficult to try to keep up with the manufacturing of them. That's where the U. S. came in. We just poured the planes in along with pilots.

The British evolved tactics that helped to support each other. These tactics kept the German planes off the backs of the English planes while the English plane was on the back of the German plane. These tactics really started to work well for them. Germany just ran out of planes.

By this time, Hitler came up with another one of his secret weapons that he was going to win the war with. Buzz bombs that have no one flying them. They just indiscriminately landed in a city. The whole purpose was to terrorize and kill civilians. It wasn't armies against each other. This tactic was directed against the English populace to break their will. Of course, the English didn't break.

PREARRANGED TRANSMISSION IN APPROXIMATE SEQUENCE

2nd BN NET

FROM	TO	MEANING	CODE	REMARKS
ABLE	NCS	Have reached phase line one	PRIMARY	
BAKER	NCS	Have reached phase line one	PRIMARY	
ABLE & BAKER	NCS	Have reached phase line two	DUPLICATE	
ABLE & BAKER	NCS	Have reached phase line three	TRIO	
CHARLIE	NCS	Mission accomplished	TARGET	
N C S	CHARLIE	JOIN Battalion	JAM	
ABLE & BAKER		Have reached "E" area	STANDFAST	
ALL S TAS.	NCS	Am in position	JELLO	
NCS	ALL STAS.	ATTACK	JUGGERNAUT	
ALL STAS.	NCS	MISSION ACCOMPLISHED	TALLYHO	

5th BN NET

FROM	TO	MEANING	CODE
ALL STAS.	NCS	HAVE REACHED PHASE LINE ONE	PRIMARY
"	"	HAVE REACHED PHASE LINE TWO	DUPLICATE
"	"	HAVE REACHED PHASE LINE THREE	TRIO
"	"	AM IN POSITION	JELLO
NCS	ALL STAS.	ATTACK	JUGGERNAUT
ALL STAS.	NCS	MISSION ACCOMPLISHED	TALLYHO

GROUP NET

FROM	TO	MEANING	CODE
NCS	ALL STAS	ASSEMBLE ON ME	ROUNDUP

CT NET
(SIMULATED)

ASSAULT NET

FROM	TO	MEANING	CODE
NCS	MAN	LAND VEHICLES AND PROCEED TO (coordinated)	SPLASH_____
MAN	NCS	HAVE LANDED - AM PROCEEDING	TOUCHDOWN

1. Radio silence will be maintained until the touch down. Units still on boats will maintain a listening watch. Transmissions will be held to those prearranged except in an emergency when the officer concerned may transmit in the clear.

2. Company commanders, with the assistance of the communications officer, will prepare their own signal plan and will submit one copy to Group Headquarters.

WIRE

1. All units will hand carry sufficient wire equipment to meet their immediate needs.

PYROTECHNIC CODE

SIGNAL	MEANING
White star parachute	Start the attack, or begin firing
Red star parachute	Cease Firing
Green star parachute	Mission accomplished
Red star cluster	Friendly troops here
Green star cluster	Need assistance

FOR THE GROUP COMMANDER

Onion skin orders sent to group commander regarding signals & radio transmissions.

Stan Askin, one of the 1st lieutenants that served with me, became a dear friend of mine after the war. He wrote down some memories. The following is one of those memories of England in the final days before D-Day.

"As time grew short we replaced the 2nd Rangers in the town of Swange on the Channel coast to practice scaling its high cliffs in preparation for our D-Day mission. Using a variety of means while under enemy fire we were to scale the sheer cliff of Pt. Du Hoc, a 100-foot promontory overlooking the crescent curve of the beach designated as Omaha and destroy the German battery of heavy casemated guns that it was feared could sweep the entire landing area and devastate the invasion forces.

"To make room for the Rangers in Swange some of the units of the 1st Division, the battle scarred "Big Red One," had been moved from their billets to a less desirable location, and away from their girlfriends. To get even we heard that some of them told the English girls that the Rangers were killers who had to have murdered at least one of their parents to qualify for the battalion.

"One evening I was in a pub sitting alone at the bar when a group of 1st Division men at a nearby table began talking loudly about how these so-called tough Rangers had never been in combat and were yet to hear a shot fired in anger. They were speaking for my benefit but I ignored them. I knew something they didn't know, that the invasion of France was scheduled for the first week in June. By then we'd all be combat veterans. A young woman in an English uniform leaned over to me and said, 'Don't let it bother you. You boys will get your chance.'"

We were aboard ship just prior to the invasion and witnessed a German raid on English cities. The search lights in the night sky finally pin-pointed the buzz bomb, like a moth caught in a flashlight way up high. And then the damnedest Fourth of July thing we'd ever seen in our lives. Tracer ammunition went up as they traced the shots. The sky was just alive with bursts.

OMAHA BEACH
1944

DEBARQUEMENT EN NORMANDIE
6 JUIN 1944
OMAHA BEACH
Les troupes US abordent la plage.
Plan du secteur OMAHA BEACH

NORMANDY LANDINGS
6-6-1944
OMAHA BEACH
US Infantry land on the beach.
Map of OMAHA BEACH sector

Commemorative Postcard

Chapter Six

The Landing

There was only one mission for the Rangers for the invasion of Normandy—to secure Pointe du Hoc.
—Ace Parker

OUR ACTIONS WERE laid out on a sand mock-up. It included every possible detail, down to the telephone posts. Villages with six or seven houses were all on there. Every detail. Every man in the company was responsible to learn every move that was going to be made by them as well as every one else's moves. It was the big adventure of our lives. To walk up and down the road as an infantryman, they didn't always know what was going on. But as a Ranger we knew exactly what was going on, even where everyone was, particularly as a company commander.

Nearly every natural science was applied to the invasion's success. Hydrographers looked at the tides and assessed what was covered during low tide, what wasn't. It was studied down to the nitty gritty. In the mean time, they got good contact with the French Underground, which was very helpful. The Underground kept track of freight moving back and forth across Germany, and in which direction. They kept track of supplies, the coming and going of the trains. They also monitored the morale of the German troops, their quality and where they were.

There was only one mission for the Rangers for the invasion of Normandy—to secure Pointe du Hoc and the guns that were on Pointe du Hoc. These were huge guns, 155 mm canon. They could cover both Omaha and Utah Beaches visually from the Pointe and particularly from the gun control spot located on the Pointe. The guns were in what looked like a huge pillbox. They could also cover out to sea ten to twelve miles and hit any ship there. So they had to be taken out. A plan was evolved. That was the only assignment for the Rangers—Pointe du Hoc. If one platoon could have done it, fine. But they had to have enough men to back up several alternate plans.

Hitler was positive that this was not going to be the area for the invasion. The tides were too high and it was farther away from England than at other points. He appointed Rommell, the "Desert Fox," to handle the whole thing. Rommell came out and was appalled at the lack of defenses in this area. He got in almost a year of building to reinforce it.

Hitler's micro-management of his army cost him a lot on D-Day. Hitler had two regiments of tanks and tank commanders just sitting there about two miles back ready to repulse a landing at Normandy or Calais. The generals in charge of them could not go when the invasion came because the order to do so had to come from Hitler. Hitler was taking a nap and they were too afraid to wake him. If they had hit us when the invasion came they could have rolled us right back into the sea.

On D-Day we Rangers had two battalions with six companies each. Three companies of the 2nd, (D, E, and F) went in first on Pointe du Hoc with the mission to take out the big guns. This was the group that you read so much about. The 2nd Battalion Commander, Lt. Col. James Rudder, was told not to go in with the first wave. They didn't want him shot up. The task was simple but extremely dangerous. They wanted one of the other officers, a captain, to lead the invasion. But Rudder told the generals that if he didn't go in, he couldn't guarantee that the Pointe would be taken. So he went in with them.

The whole 5th Battalion and two companies of the 2nd Battalion went in on Omaha Beach. Our mission was to follow

Rudder's 2nd Battalion Rangers and climb the cliff behind them. We were to first receive a signal that they had secured the Pointe. If no signal was received we were to come in to the Pointe from the land side—enter at Omaha Beach and go inland and then make a right hand turn, approaching the Pointe from the South, or inland side.

C Company with the 2nd Battalion had a different mission, it's own separate target. They were to take out the radar and guns built right into the edge of the cliffs to the west, on the Pointe de la Percee. This was C Company's job, and it was a nasty one. A bunch of Germans were there firing right down on top of them. They lost a lot of men there but succeeded in their mission.

According to the morning reports I still have in my possession from June 1944, on the third of June, D-Day was announced for 5 June, 1944, H-Hour (Hour of Invasion) at 0610. On 4 June, D-Day was postponed to 6 June with H-Hour at 0630. At 1630 (4:30 PM) both ships hoisted anchor and joined the convoy in the channel. The 5th Ranger Battalion left Dorchester, England, by vehicle at 0700 and arrived in Weymouth, England, at 0939. From there they boarded LCAs, left Weymouth Harbor and arrived at and boarded the H.M.S. Leopold, Boudouin and the Prince Charles at 1045.

My company, A Company, 5th Rangers, boarded the Leopold, a coastal freighter that had been used up and down the channel. I think it was a Belgium ship. The invasion was called for June 5th, but was delayed due to a storm. We stayed in port. If the weather got any milder at all, then we were going to have to go, because we had everybody assembled. So it wasn't a very long delay.

When it was time to load for the beach landings they announced, "Man your boats. Attention on deck! United States Rangers, man your boats." Then everybody reported to a particular assault boat and got into his assigned spot. Stan

Askin, a good friend of mine in recent years, wrote some thoughts in 1990 about boarding the LCA boats. The following is his memory of that day.

When an F Company man came in at 0400 to wake John (my cabin mate), I was sound asleep. John shook me awake and left the cabin. But now craving sleep, I figured I could grab a few more winks because I didn't have any men to supervise. Since Scotland I had been the assistant to Major Sullivan, the 5th Battalion's Executive Officer and S-3 and was only responsible for getting myself to the landing crafts suspended from the Baudouin's upper deck. The implications of what happened next were buried in my subconscious for decades. I suddenly came awake with a start, not knowing what time it was or how long I had slept. Sitting bolt upright in a panic, I glanced at my watch and saw that almost a half hour had passed. Outside all was silence. In sheer horror I thrust my feet into my boots, hooked on my ammunition belt holding my Colt '45, my ammunition clips, compass, grenades and canteen, flung on my jacket and backpack, picked up my Thompson submachine gun, my helmet, my gas mask and my Mae West (life preserver), raced out of the cabin and down the ship's empty corridors to the upper deck. Running down the deck in the dark, my heart pumping, I could see some of the LCAs already in the water bobbing on the waves and others being lowered over the side, but I couldn't find my staff boat. Then at the last possible moment I recognized it as it began to descend and I leaped over the side crashing down on several of the men. Fortunately, neither Lt. Col. Schneider or Major Sullivan witnessed my embarrassing and belated entry.

It was now just past 0430, and I'll never know what

woke me in the nick of time. Another minute or two and I would have been standing on the deck watching my Ranger battalion fade into the dark. To avoid that disgrace I would have jumped overboard, equipment and all, and tried to swim for shore 12 miles away. And as the creaking winches dropped us into the choppy water in the cold predawn gloom, the very British voice of the ship's captain came over the public address system, 'Good hunting, Rangers!' This expression of a certain class of Briton's sporting attitude toward war suddenly brought me wide awake, forcing me to confront, for the first time, the terrible truth that I was quite possibly facing the last couple hours of my life. I felt an icy horror colder than the briny swells in which we now tossed and bobbed.

We had gone through the drill. Every man was fully equipped for combat. Captain. John C. Raaen, Jr. described the Ranger gear in his book, *Sir, The 5ᵗʰ Rangers Have Landed Intact:*

> The standard equipment for a Ranger consisted of helmet and helmet liner, with some wearing the wool knit cap under the helmet. Most stuffed toilet paper into the harness of the helmet liner. The helmets had no covers or netting. The battle dress was an impregnated, olive drab, fatigue type uniform. The cloth was stiff and smelled from the impregnation that was designed to reduce chemical warfare casualties should the Germans use toxic chemicals. Field jackets and stripped packs were next, together with the rifle belt and its suspenders. Most men armed with the M-1 Rifle carried two bandoleers of extra rifle ammunition. Two to four grenades were taped to the suspenders. Most of the grenades were fragmentation,

but a sprinkling were smoke and thermite. A bayonet and entrenching tool were attached to the pack. A poncho and personal articles were carried in the pack. First aid packs with morphine syringes, a fighting knife, lensatic compass, and canteen were attached to the belt. A gas mask and one or two inflatable life belts (affectionately referred to as "Mae Wests") hung around the waist. Three days worth of D rations were carried in the pack. (D bars are concentrated chocolate with a lot of calories. These were separate from the rest of the rations and heavily wrapped in foil.) Many wore wrist watches, and carried field glasses and a Caliber .45, M1911A1 automatic pistol. Bloused trousers and jump boots completed the array. Cavalry type blanket rolls with the rest of the Rangers personal equipment, were stored with the rear echelon.

Each person carried their own ammunition and the weapons they would need as soon as their feet hit the sand. Supply would have the excess. Everybody that went in was really, really loaded.

The LCAs were swung out and lowered over the side of the ship on davits according to a schedule. These were pulleys attached to the small boats on each end. The LCAs were lined up one after another, covering both sides of the mother ship. Each LCA held about 35 men. They were made of steel. We had learned our lesson from the Dieppe Raid. There they had gone in using wooden boats and enemy machine gun fire had just chopped them to pieces on the way in.

Three benches lined the inside of the boats. One along each of the sides and one center bench. My Squad Sergeant, Hathaway, remembers some details about the LCAs:

"On the middle bench we would sit straddle leg. The guys on the side boards had it the worst as they had to face inboard, and of course with the equipment on their backs they were up against the side of the boat. I would say there were 11 or 12 men on a bench. I was seated first man on the middle board, Ace was on my left and Souchier was on my right. We knew exactly where we were going to be seated as we had a lot of rehearsals. The LCAs were lowered to deck level so we could mount them right from the deck by walking right on, about five or six at a time.

"The battleship Texas was on our right side, its bow into us. They dropped anchor. Then His Majesty's heavy cruiser, the Glasgow, pulled in on our starboard side with its bow also into us. And they dropped anchor. They, then, fired broadside. Well, that Texas, when she fired, the recoil was so great, the back rail of the battleship went right into the water. We could see the shells going in. They were red hot going through the air. So we were watching all this happening as we were going in. It was one hellacious noise! I've never heard anything like it. Believe it or not, it gave you a rather firm belief that it was going to be all right going in. And that wasn't all. Even the tanks as they were going in were elevated so they could fire right from their boats. Artillery pieces on the boats going in were also raised up so they could fire. Everything was firing! So, with all this stuff going off, you figure this isn't going to be bad."

The English coxswains in the assault boat carrying the 2nd Battalion Rangers and LTC. Rudder were headed for the promontory where C Company was to attack, and not for the Pointe. They had made a mistake. That would have put them somewhere midpoint between the Pointe and Omaha Beach. By the time they made the correction, it had cost enough time so that the signal for us to help them on the Pointe was delayed. It came too late for us to join them. So we improvised.

The 2nd Battalion's plan was to get in with the boats at the base of the cliffs and get the ropes up to aid in climbing to the cliff top. They used grappling hooks for this, tied to the end of a rope. They would shoot the grappling hooks out of mortars. It turned out that the ropes were absolutely soaked and therefore weighed about 10 to 20 times more than usual. Many of them never reached the tops when they fired them out of the tubes. A few did. In addition to a few ladders, many of the guys also attacked the sheer cliff with just climbing skills. It was a ragged cliff so there were lots of holes to grab. They used their trench knives or their bayonets to stab into the ground to hold them as they climbed and used whatever—their teeth, eyebrows!

They climbed the Pointe on both sides, wherever they could. There was no waiting. You're taught as a Ranger never to stand still—always keep moving. They knew what they needed to do. But when they reached the top, they found telephone poles had been substituted for the big guns that they were to take out. They found tracks leading out of the casemates. Thinking these tracks were made by the guns, Sgts. Leonard Lomell and Jack Kuhn followed them. About one kilometer inland they found them ready to fire in the direction of Utah Beach, with piles of ammunition around them. They unhesitatingly placed thermite grenades in the recoil and traversing mechanisms of two of the guns, disabling them. The 2nd Rangers had completed their mission.

What we later found out was that a French farmer in the FFI, Free French Intelligence, rode by there and realized there were no guns on the Pointe. This FFI agent had just one more day before he could reach a place where there was a clandestine radio to transmit the information back over to England. Since he knew nothing about the plans for D-Day, he thought he had plenty of time. If we had known the guns had been moved, we probably wouldn't have mounted our attack there.

I remember transports kept pouring the goods in on D-Day. The air force was flying over. The Germans, in contrast, only had one plane seen that day. The Allies tried to plant their bombs just behind the cliff to avoid bombing their own troops hitting the beach. They went out wrong, probably due to bad weather, and bombed twenty miles behind the beach. So they were no help. We found out that the artillery from the smaller ships, the cruisers and such, didn't do as much damage to the defenses as they thought they would.

Lt. Col. Max Schneider was our commanding officer of the Fifth Ranger Battalion on D-Day. James Graves, Jr., a Tech 4 with the Headquarters Company and in the same LCA as Schneider, has this memory:

> "The first indication that we had been seen was when a large artillery shell landed in the water about 100 feet to the side of the landing craft I was in. At that point, Colonel Schneider ordered all the men to stand up and look straight ahead. 'That is where you are going to land. Now get down and don't for any reason stand up again!'"

The 29th Division, 116th regiment had been ahead of us in one sector of the beach. Where we went in, the whole 5th Battalion and two companies of the 2nd Battalion hit Omaha Beach together. The Pointe itself had been a target for anything that the Allies could throw at it for a long time.

Months before that, the Air Force had been sent over it to drop bombs. They sent ships out there to stand 10 to 15 miles and lob huge shells in there. They were firing at a target that was 100 feet high. They didn't want to get the shells too far over the cliff and have them land to hell and gone someplace inland. They wanted them to just clear the cliff edge so that the shells would land directly on the Pointe.

As we faced it coming in, the Pointe is to the right, or the west. South is directly inland from the water. Omaha was to the East and not very far from the Pointe. Utah was just to the other side of the Pointe. We came in at low tide so there was a beach in front of the Pointe.

The first scene in *Saving Private Ryan* was what happened to the 29th Division. We hit the beach and lost only a fraction of what the 29th Division had even though we were only 100 yards from them.

Colonel Max Schneider could see what was happening to the 29th Division on the beach where we were to land. The beach was getting blasted. He decided to turn further east.

Herb Epstein, Max Schneider's Intelligence Sergeant, can recall vividly landing on Omaha Beach.

> "We landed at Dog White. I was in the lead boat and by Schneider's side the whole time. Schneider, by the way, was my god. Max to me was the savior of not only the 5th Ranger Battalion on D-Day but of the entire sector of Omaha Beach. It wasn't just guts, it was combat savvy. He was the only one of the two Ranger Battalions to have combat experience. We were in the front of the lead boat together and he saw what was happening on the beach when we started to go in. He ordered the flotilla commander to turn the boat to the left and go parallel to the beach to an area that looked like it wasn't so heavy. He told the flotilla commander to get us in and get us in fast. And he did! He got us in pretty good shape. He just made the decision and gave the order. Max was very direct. Max knew exactly what to do!"

So we went in. But before we even reached the shore, we had to go through a maze of deadly underwater obstacles. The engineers had been here ahead of us and had cleared some lanes in to the beach for our boats to land. But what remained was still terrific. Great logs or poles were positioned at a slant, pointing up and out towards our incoming boats. They had mines attached so that if we hit them with any force it was going to knock us out of commission. It was an obstacle course. The Germans had masses of great six-pronged spiders—made of railroad iron and standing shoulder-high— just beneath the surface of the water. These were criss-crossed and anchored deep into the sand. They stood as a tripod and were extremely sturdy. In addition to these obstacles they had floating mines off shore, land mines buried in the sand of the beach, and more mines in rows waiting in the tall grass and bluffs beyond the sand.

Hathaway, my Squad Sergeant mentioned earlier, recalls coming in on the beach:

> "The coxswain steered the boat. The coxswain's head was above the boat. He needed to steer around the mines sticking out of the water on posts. Also on each boat were the chief of the boat, an engineer, and two men running the anchor. The boat had an anchor at the rear. Just before landing they dropped the anchor. A small motor ran the winch on the anchor. Even if it landed right up on the sand of the beach, the motor was so powerful that it could drag the boat back off to return to the mother ship. And of course the boat became lighter when it lost 32 men and their equipment. Just figure that (evacuation) of each man running 175 pounds of his own weight plus 100 pounds of equipment, would allow the boat to suddenly ride higher in the water. That's how we lost one man, Pfc. Chester A. Tarlano—the boat ran over him. He was the last one out of the other boat carrying the rest of

Company A. He didn't jump far enough away from the boat and was pulled under.

"But what a hell of a surprise we were in for. What was supposed to be all blown apart, wasn't. The Germans had their dugouts so deep it was almost impervious to artillery fire. As we were going in, we were getting machine-gun fire and some mortar and artillery fire from the German guns. You'd be surprised how much you remember of your training when a bullet flies by your head. All I could think was, 'My God, you're never going to make it across that beach alive!' That's how bad it was!"

Both our units were in relatively good condition after the landings and we had suffered only minor losses, but the men were crowded shoulder to shoulder, sometimes several rows deep, along the shingle at the base of the timber sea wall. Francis Coughlin with the Headquarters unit of the 5th recalls:

"People were dying on the beach because they had no place to go; they were afraid to go. We were taught during all our training that you never stand still. You must move. If you move you have a better chance of living. However, we were never in the place we were supposed to be. I was there and should have been over here. They were here and supposed to be over there."

Herb Epstein remembers what happened at the sea wall:

"Max and I were at the beach wall, prone, and Cota came strolling down the beach upright and came over to us. (General Cota was the assistant commander of the 29th Infantry Division and was the first American general ashore on D-Day.) Max then went ahead and stood upright too. Cota said, 'I'm counting on you Rangers to lead the way.' Then Cota left and Max dropped down again. I said to Max, 'What the hell were you doing?' 'If he was standing, I wasn't going to be laying down here!' Max replied."

I also remember that moment. Cota came strolling down the beach and said, "Lead the way, Rangers, my men are green." Well, we were inexperienced, too. Cota was inquiring "What unit are you?" and "We have to get off this beach now." He was moving along from group to group. Cota was an old timer, someone to greatly admire.

The 1st Platoon of A Company and myself had successfully crossed the beach, traversed a farmer's field using a drainage ditch, and finally reached the chateau and farmhouse, our first rendezvous point. Out of 560 men, only 23 had gotten there. But we had more challenges ahead of us. Our long day had only just begun.

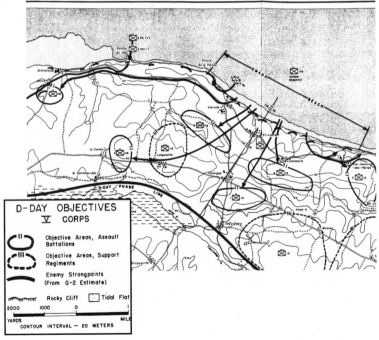

Source: Omaha Beachhead, American Forces in Action Series, Historical Division, War Dept., 1945

"It was the adventure of a lifetime if you could live through it!"

—"Ace" Parker

Chapter Seven

Hedgerow Fighting

Oh, my Lord, I've never heard such a nice sound in all my life as an American asking me what the password was! So I gave it: "Tallyho!"
—Ace Parker

NO ONE ELSE was at the Chateau except for a couple of regular soldiers gathered in a group of trees to the side. No one had seen the rest of the Ranger Battalion. Considering the amount of time we were on our bellies in that ditch, I imagined that the rest of my Ranger Battalion had been there and gone on, not being able to wait for us. It also occurred to me that I had virtually no knowledge as to the well-being or successes of the rest of my battalion. I knew they had gotten off the beach but knew nothing of what had happened to them since. We had been functioning on our own now for many hours. The last time I saw my group had been at the beach. And that was literally a mess.

So we took off. We figured that maybe we'd catch them, not knowing what was ahead. This time we were following a secondary road between two high ridges of the old plant fences or hedgerows. The French didn't use wire fences. Rocks and earth piled up in a long row formed a barrier, joined with trees and shrubs and everything else that had grown in over several hundred years. This made for a dense wall. Every so often there would be a small opening in the hedgerow to move the farmer's machinery or cows from one field to another. These were dangerous spots as the Germans had a lot of guns directed on these openings. This was the

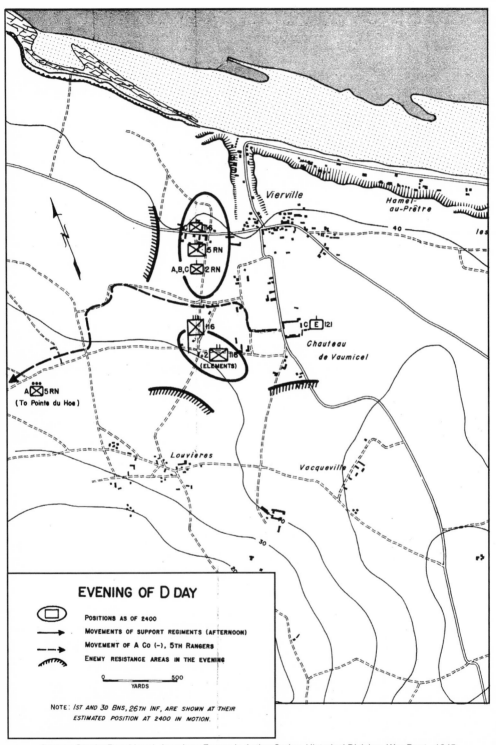

Vierville

Hamel-
au-Prêtre

les

40

116

5 RN

A,B,C 2 RN

C E 121

116

Chauteau
de Vaumicel

2 116
(ELEMENTS)

A 5 RN
(To Pointe du Hoe)

Louvières

Vacqueville

30

EVENING OF D DAY

POSITIONS AS OF 2400

MOVEMENTS OF SUPPORT REGIMENTS (AFTERNOON)

MOVEMENT OF A Co (-), 5TH RANGERS

ENEMY RESISTANCE AREAS IN THE EVENING

0   500
          YARDS

NOTE: 1ST AND 3D BNS, 26TH INF, ARE SHOWN AT THEIR
      ESTIMATED POSITION AT 2400 IN MOTION.

Source: Omaha Beachhead, American Forces in Action Series, Historical Division, War Dept., 1945

hedgerow country.

We would jump around and sometimes we would use farmer's trails—some of them were wide enough for a wagon, some of them just wide enough to carry a bicycle. We were jumping around following a hedgerow for a while then jumping to another one. We were using our compasses. We weren't worried about mines. They were on the coastal areas.

The dirt roads appeared as tunnels located between the hedgerows. We were following a secondary road when we started running into pockets of German soldiers—a dozen here, six there. There would be a sharp little fire fight. We would either knock them out completely or pick up some prisoners. We had a considerable number of prisoners actually, 20 or so. We were making a lot of noise as we went along, having to overcome a lot of Germans.

We had disarmed the prisoners as we captured them by throwing their rifles over the hedgerows. I had told my men previously that if a man is disarmed then he is not to be shot. That would be murder. I didn't want to hear about anyone killing a prisoner that had already been disarmed. Prisoners, however, can be a hindrance. We were not equipped to handle them, at least not with the few men and limited equipment we had. Our objective as Rangers was to carry out a specific mission; it was not to take prisoners along the way.

Nearing a French hamlet that the Germans had been occupying, we were running into more and more resistance from the Germans. Soon, we ran into a much larger pocket of Germans. It became apparent as we were walking along the road that we were nearly surrounded. We could hear the Germans talking on either side of the hedgerows. Realizing that we were there, they started to throw their "potato mashers" over the hedgerows at us. (The German grenades were called potato mashers by the Americans as they looked like a regular potato masher—there was a wooden handle for throwing and a bulky end that was the actual grenade.) We would pick up the potato mashers by their long handles and throw them back at the Germans. We found them easier to throw than our own grenades.

Sometimes these devices would go off and sometimes they wouldn't. The Germans used the Polish and others from conquered countries to work in their factories making whatever they needed. There was talk that the slave labor had sabotaged a lot of the grenades, so a lot of times they were blanks and just didn't fire.

We decided we needed to get out of there and right now. If we waited too much longer they would pinch behind us and easily capture us. We couldn't keep going forward, however, since it was apparent that there were too many Germans ahead. We still had the prisoners with us, so we told them, "Get out of here!" I was not going to murder them. They had no guns.

We communicated the plan amongst us with very little words, mostly hand signals. Then we bugged out, quickly running 100 yards back along the road from where we had just come. I mean we really ran. I don't know what happened to our prisoners as I never looked back to find out. We wanted to clear those German soldiers as fast as we could. When we estimated we had gone far enough, we climbed over the hedgerow towards the side of the sea. This direction would take us to the Pointe.

We took off across country then, leaving the secondary road. In the front of our group was our company's scout or point man and then his backup man. We cautiously moved forward, calculating carefully the status of the area. Time passed. It was now 9 'o clock. (Two hours of daylight remained.) Up until that time I had wondered, "Are we all that's left?" We were inland away from the Channel and heard no battle sounds on Omaha.

Suddenly an English-speaking voice challenged us, its owner well hidden in the bushes. "What's the password?"

We had come upon the outpost line of the 2nd Rangers guarding the Pointe, on the other side of the tar road. Oh, my Lord, I've never heard such a nice sound in all my life as an American asking me what the password was! So I gave it: "Tallyho!"

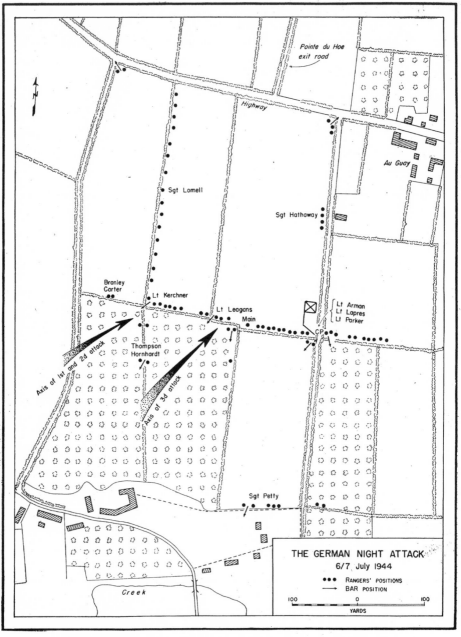

Pointe du Hoe
exit road

Highway

Au Guay

Sgt Lomell

Sgt Hathaway

Branley
Carter

Lt Kerchner

Lt Leagans

Main

Lt Arman
Lt Lapres
Lt Parker

CP

Thompson
Hornhardt

Axis of 1st and 2d attack

Axis of 3d attack

Sgt Petty

THE GERMAN NIGHT ATTACK
6/7 July 1944

●●● RANGERS' POSITIONS
→ BAR POSITION

100   0   100
YARDS

Creek

MAP NO. 8

Source: Small Unit Actions, Historical Division, War Dept., Washington, DC

Chapter Eight

D-Day Night Attack

Survival was the only thing on our minds.
—Ace Parker

THE WORD WAS sent back to Rudder that we were there. He immediately sent a message back. "Where are the rest of them?" I replied back, "I don't know. I thought they were here. They must be right behind me." But of course they weren't. The 5th and the rest of the 2nd Ranger Battalions were held up on the coastal road from Vierville su Mer headed for Grand Camp le Bain and Cherbourg, pinned down by the Germans. They would not make it through to us until two days after D-Day (D-Day+2). They had been grabbed by the superior officers of the 29th Division and were used to help take the town of Vierville. That was not our mission. However, Schneider could hardly refuse a full colonel and a general.

Lt. Stan Askin was among the group held up at the Vierville road. This is his memory of D-Day night:

> "Around midnight on June 6, as I was trying to get some sleep on the warm stone kitchen hearth of the farmhouse that we had made our command post, the battalion Executive Officer, Major Richard Sullivan, sent for me. He told me that our beachhead was so shallow that enemy snipers and interdicting artillery fire had prevented the setting up of an ammunition dump on the beach. The 'three-day' supply of ammo

we had carried in on our backs was almost exhausted, and the company commanders were pleading for more, especially mortar shells. So it was that I was to take a patrol from Headquarters Company and return to the beach to search the dead bodies for ammunition.

"We left the farmyard with a hastily recruited old French man and his horse and wagon and headed back down the dark road toward the Vierville intersection: a dozen men spread out and quiet, alert for possible ambush by Nazi infiltrators more familiar with the terrain than we, while our impressed allies, man and beast, clomped and creaked along, noisily heralding our approach with every step.

"The night air felt oppressive against my face. My breathing was easy but there was a tenseness in my legs. This was France, the German army was all around us, and the war was finally real. I would never have to wonder again about the nature of actual combat. In one long, hideous day I had become a veteran of foreign wars with comrades to mourn and bloody tales to tell my grandchildren. I considered our meager toehold and thought of the endless miles that stretched out before us across western Europe. I hoped the Russians were doing well in the East.

"Half-way to the junction we were suddenly challenged from beyond the road by an M.P. crouched in the dark. I could see his armband and the outline of his helmet. After I gave the countersign, his voice returned, nervously, 'Keep it low, men, there're Krauts all over the goddamn place here.'

"We passed a solitary tank cautiously moving up to join the perimeter. Then we were in Vierville and started down the beach road, between the high cliffs that had enabled the enemy to shoot down our throats all that morning. It was only a short walk down the beach, but before we got there an officer stepped out of a quarry and identified himself as Major Gerhardt, commander of the 29th Division. He asked what outfit I was with and inquired anxiously about the state of things "up there." I told him that the Rangers were dug in in defensive positions and that some of his men were with us. Reassured that we were holding firm, he allowed my little party to proceed and returned to his quarry.

"At the bottom of the draw was the beach, and along the beach, shoulder to shoulder, partly submerged by the tide, were the bodies. They stretched as far as I could see in the dim light afforded by anti-aircraft searchlights located on ships anchored out in the Channel and the glow from a large Landing Craft Infantry that had been burning since early morning.

"The dead lay under the stars, the water lapping at their feet. They lay on the road behind the beach. And scattered among them, still grasping the attenuated thread of life after eighteen hours of poorly administered pain and agony, were the wounded, who surely felt abandoned by God and man.

"We started down the beach, past a group of "walking wounded" who huddled in the meager shelter of a cliff, tended by a few bone-tired aid men whose medical kits were empty long since of their small supplies of morphine, sulfa, styrettes, bandages and splints. With involuntary patience they awaited the dawn and the coming of the Medical Corps.

"As we passed beyond this point, there came out of the gloom weak and pathetic cries for water and morphine from men whose internal wounds forbade either simple comfort as a direct threat to flickering life. We made these men as comfortable as we could with whatever was at hand and hoped they had enough remaining endurance to last out the night.

"The lethal, roaming searchlights scanned the dark sky for stray Luftwaffe bombers venturing over the landing area now that darkness had sent our air cover back to English bases. The LCI burned in the distance, eerily illuminating some of the human and material wreckage that strewed the beach. We heard sporadic firing from our perimeter. And then we knelt at the water's edge and began going over the dead bodies of our buddies for ammunition they had never had a chance to fire but might keep some of the rest of us alive. I opened the back pack of the first man I came to and on top was a Jewish prayer book similar to the one my aunt gave me the morning I boarded a train for Camp Lee, Virginia, the first stop on the journey that led to Omaha Beach. A book I had never opened."

There were three officers and their men from the 2nd Battalion Rangers at the outpost line, which was across the highway from the Pointe. Rudder was at the Command Post on the Pointe itself. They needed my men to reinforce the outpost line. So they took my men. It sounded sensible—not to take over a section of the line ourselves, but to strengthen the line. The 2nd Battalion Rangers had already been in the position for some time. We were a welcome sight to those struggling to hold onto the outpost line.

So they dispersed us among Rudder's men. Some of them were in foxholes along the hedgerows. A foxhole was built as deep as you could get it provided you have the time to dig and the ground is diggable. You get down as far as you can so that you can crouch or stand to shoot.

Since they had been there for some hours already, and knew the lay of the land, they positioned my men to help hold the sector just south of Pointe du Hoc. The officers of the 2nd

Battalion assigned my men positions along the field dividing them into groups of two or three.

I was positioned at the Command Post—the CP—which lay at the southeast corner of the field. Night fell. It was pitch black. It was difficult to see anything. Then the Germans came in with enormous firepower and noise. Confusion followed.

It was important to Colonel Rudder to maintain the block on the Grandcamp Highway and so deny access of that vital road to the enemy. The main indications for enemy strength lay to the South (inland) and West of the Pointe. We took up positions to guard this sector. A couple of men here and there were positioned along the hedgerows and at the corners to hold this position. My 23 men were scattered and did not function as a tactical unit.

Men in foxholes were stationed together in twos for greater safety in night fighting. We also had 30-40 prisoners that we placed into foxholes and guarded them. Our main worry was our reduced ammunition supply and lack of food. Many of us had eaten only D-bars. However, survival was the only thing on our minds at this time.

Lieutenant Kerchner reported that he had seen Germans of some strength to the southwest. Sergeant Petty was positioned with a couple of men at an outpost located furthest south of the group. He was told to withdraw if an attack developed in his vicinity. At the bottom of the little valley ran a country road almost parallel to our lines. In daylight, it was easy to watch this road for enemy movement, but at night the road was hard to see.

Close by in an orchard, machine gun fire from the Germans followed an outburst of their whistles and shouts. A second round of machine gun fire came from the west. One man was killed by a grenade and another was hit in the shoulder with a bullet. Somehow, he managed to crawl to the cover of a hedgerow. In another outpost, a couple of men were nearly walked over by a group of Germans who suddenly came around a hump in the hedgerow. Corporal Thompson saw their silhouettes against the sky and was able to get in the first fire at point-blank range, bringing down three of the enemy. The other Germans in the group hit the ground and threw grenades. One exploded in Thompson's face, cutting him badly. He gave his BAR (Browning Automatic Rifle) to Hornhardt and they retreated to the corner. Once reaching the corner they found no one at this position. They called out for Sergeant Rupinski and got no reply. He was 20 yards away but did not hear them call out. There were two D Company men close by with a BAR but Thompson missed seeing them too. Assuming that everyone had pulled back, they headed north along D Company's hedgerow. They passed others along the way in foxholes but did not see them either.[2] It was that dark!

Lt. Kerchner and Sgt. Fate had received the greatest concentration of enemy fire at their position. Determining that the attack was going to roll right over them, they decided to move further north and withdraw along the hedgerow. Kerchner called to his men to follow as he was running north along the hedgerow, but no one heard him. Only two men joined us at the highway. Two men appeared at the CP and told Lt. Arman that they had been told to withdraw. No one knew where this order had come from.

Down near the creek, at Sergeant Petty's exposed outpost, he thought he might have heard "clinking sounds" coming from the farm buildings located close by. After a short spell of quiet, a machine gun opened up from that flank. Some shots ricocheted off a farm roller that Petty had placed to the right of his location for protection. Petty and his group stayed quiet and soon the firing stopped. Following earlier instructions, Petty decided to pull back to the CP. His group made the trip without further skirmish.[3]

Two men were sent out to pass the word to expect more attacks. These men were to also check the functioning of weapons and look for casualties. The group of German prisoners were moved to a more central location and told to dig in for their own safety.

About 0100 the Germans attacked with a stronger effort, hitting again from the South and Southwest. The Germans had stealthily gotten through the orchard and to within 50 yards of us. The attack opened with whistles and a sort of "roll call" as the Germans shouted their names up and down the line. We figured it was meant to intimidate us.

At 0300 another attack developed by the Germans. There was a great deal of fire and most of it was indirect, which had the result of confusing us. One fox hole had Pfc. Main in it, wounded by a grenade. Main could hear the Germans coming up close in the wheat just on the other side of the hedgerow. After hearing one of the American's BAR go silent, he crawled in amongst the briars and got himself into the middle of the hedgerow. Next he could hear Staff Sgt. Simmons surrendering to the Germans, as he lay hidden, only 15 feet away. The Germans came no further East and thus did not find him.[4]

Burnett was in a fox hole some 25 yards east of the corner. Near Burnett, the Germans had worked through the orchard close to the men positioned there, and their automatic fire ripped through the hedgerow, keeping the men down. Some of the Rangers used German grenades of which we had plenty, in a close-range exchange. Burnett realized that Sergeant Bogetto's BAR to his left, had gone silent. A burst of German fire, sweeping along the German side of the hedge, hit their foxholes. Burnett and the man next to him were wounded. He could hear Sergeant Rupinski arguing with a few Rangers, trying to decide whether they could fight it out. The talk ended with Rupinski shouting, "Kamerad." The Germans moved in and rounded up the survivors, many of them wounded, including Burnett. Lieutenant Leagans was dead[5]. (Burnett, who escaped a few days later by killing a guard, was assisted by the French Underground and succeeded in getting back to the Allied lines, but not until August.)

Evidently a hasty decision to withdraw was planned by a few, but not all of us. As the volume of fire built up, hasty measures were taken to pass the word around to withdraw back to the highway and the Pointe. Some of us failed to get the notice and were temporarily left behind. Noncommissioned officers tried hurriedly to round up their men. Once started, movement was fast. My staff sergeant, Hathaway, had been posted halfway back to the highway along the lane. His first notice of what was happening came when he saw men running by to the north. Hathaway said he stuck his head through the hedgerow and shouted, "Hey! What's up? Where are you going?" The nearest man stopped running, put his rifle in Hathaway's face, and demanded the password. Hathaway was so rattled that he could just remember the word in time. He was then told, "The Germans are right behind us. Get out quick to the Pointe." He collected part of his group and went north; the others he couldn't find, but they came in later. The prisoners were left behind.

As we arrived at the blacktop there was no sign of pursuit. We made an effort to reorganize. My men had made their way through the unfamiliar terrain in scattered groups back to the highway. They resented being left behind—I vowed we would never be separated again.

Some dozen men of Company D's contingent had no notice of the withdrawal and remained in their original positions along the hedgerow. When they realized what had happened, they had no chance to retreat as the Germans were too close. They remained there that night and all of the following day. They were not able to be freed until the morning of the following day when the 116th Infantry moved in.

On the east-west hedgerow three more Rangers had been left behind in the confusion. Main was one. Another, Theobald, had been left behind in the field guarding the prisoners. During the final attack he came over to Main to help out. He could find no Rangers, but heard German voices so he hid in the ditch. Wadsworth, 75 yards from Main, had also missed the word of withdrawal. When he finally called to his neighbor who had only been a few yards away, he received no answer. He stayed put under a tangle of briars.

We found out later that both Theobold and Wadsworth were caught during the next two days. Wadsworth was spotted the next morning. The following morning on D+2, Theobold heard firing close to his hideout. He did not know that this was the 116th attacking to relieve the Pointe. Trying to reach his group again, Theobold left the highway and was cutting south when he was captured by a German machine gun post. Main spent D+1 watching German patrols go by. He watched as the Germans set up a machine gun. That night he threw a grenade in the direction of the machine gun and "lit out" for the Pointe without drawing enemy fire.[6]

On D+1 our force headed by Colonel Rudder consisted of about 90 men able to bear arms. We were expecting heavy assault. With the support of the strong naval fire, which had kept us alive for two days, we did hold out. That afternoon we received food, ammunition and a reinforcement of men that had landed on the beach below. I remember one man, Otto Masney, a solidly built soldier with the 2nd Rangers. In a sheer show of strength and defiance, he stood upon the Pointe, raised his rifle with one arm high above his head and gave a mighty yell: "Germans, come and get us!" It was a fierce challenge of Ranger spirit. That was a sight I'll never forget: Otto, standing on the cliff, alone, silhouetted against the sky.

Chapter Nine

Along the Cliff Edge

We thought maybe the whole invasion had failed.
This made us plenty scared.

—Ace Parker

IT WAS NOW 0400. Lt. Rudder felt that we should try to find where the rest of the 5th Ranger Battalion and 2nd Ranger Battalion were located. They were pretty damn desperate up on the Pointe. They were running out of food, ammunition, water and everything else. The batteries were gone on the radios. Eichner, the communications officer, was down to using "semi-four"—using flags to form letters so that he could pass messages. He was relaying to the ships in the harbor needs of the troops and asking for reinforcements. The ships had contact with all the people along the coast line that had working radios. We could go through the ships to communicate to higher headquarters in the corps. Eichner was able to get the message out that they needed ammunition, batteries for the radios, and that they had a lot of casualties that needed to be taken off.

The plan was made for us to try to reach the beach and travel along it to Vierville. We thought the rest might be held up there. Rudder assigned me to take six men to accomplish this mission. He felt going along the cliff would be a good route. I picked my men and we headed out.

Within minutes we found that we had entered a mine field. About this same time I also discovered that I had seven soldiers with me instead of six. One of the youngest and greenest soldiers had decided to join us. He did not want to be left with strangers. But now it was too late to go back. We had not noticed him following along in the dark.

We started along the cliff's edge. We had to cover a stretch of 20 yards over open ground before we could reach the cover of a small berm or rounded mound of dirt. We started our runs one person at a time. Sgt. Denzil Johnson went first and drew no fire. Pfc. Paul Peavey followed but was hit in the chest and killed by machine gun fire from somewhere inland. We kept low in a crater and fired 3 antitank grenades at the machine gun, trying to judge its location by the sound of its fire. Johnson left the berm and started crawling over open ground to circle back to the path. Some of the men thought they saw him get hit by a bullet as he crawled. My Staff Sgt. Hathaway looked out of the crater a moment later and could see somebody's foot. He called and got no answer. Johnson was given up as lost.

A burst of machine gun fire came directly on us just as Pfc. James Gabaree began crawling. He got his buttocks too far in the air and was unlucky enough to get a bullet from a German sniper. We pulled him down from the ridge and tucked him in a crevice below the cliff's edge. We gave him a canteen of water and instructed him to stay there. We told him that someone would be sent back to get him later. We'd list his location in the report of casualties. There was nothing else we could do.

It was clear that we would have to retrace our way still further back along the cliff. Our first move would take us into a large and dense patch of brush, running right to the cliff edge and exposed to enemy fire. While we were debating how to manage this, Sgt. Johnson's head poked through the brush just over the crater as he yelled, "Ace! Where the hell have you been? I've been looking for you for half an hour."

Johnson had not been hit as we had previously thought. He had found a small funnel in the field that gave him just enough cover. He crawled west 200 yards, angling back toward the cliff. Then, finding no trace of the patrol, he started again toward the crater, going along the cliff side just under the top. When he got to the brush, he was forced to go through it. It had taken him 15 minutes to negotiate 30 yards. He broke his way through the brush using only his hands, all the while keeping quiet so as not to attract enemy attention.

Johnson had proved that the brush could be traversed. We followed his trail back through the brush, crawling in single file.

On the way we were forced to travel very close to the cliff edge, which had started to dislodge in whole sections due to Naval gun fire. The second man in line, Sgt. Clyde Farrell, noticed a crack in the edge but was so scared he forgot to pass back a warning to the rest of us. Each man that crawled over that crack felt the earth give a little. By the time Hathaway, the last man in line, passed over the crack, it was a foot wide. But we passed without incident.

We decided to rest at a notch in the cliff edge. Someone suggested climbing down the cliff to the beach below in order to move faster along the sand. The beach was relatively free from German fire, and this would make a good route to get to Omaha Beach and then over to Vierville. We removed the slings from our rifles and tied them together to form a rope. We then lowered a man down as far as we could to see if he could jump the rest of the way to the sand. We got to within 40 feet of the bottom, reaching a bulge on the sloping face. But then came a vertical section with jagged rocks below, so dangerous that it prevented us from going any further.

Once on top again, we headed back along the cliff edge. Several times we were stopped by machine gun fire. We figured that an enemy patrol was moving parallel to our moves.

By mid day we were nearly north of Englesqueville and nearly half way back to the Pointe. The 18 inch berm inland from the cliff and beach served to mark the mine field for the

Germans themselves and the French who had to live there. The berm also served to protect us from incoming bullets. It wouldn't have protected us at all if the Germans were using mortars. A mortar goes up and comes straight down. But ball fire, rifle fire and machine gun fire travels on a level. With machine guns they could hit anything above that berm, but anything below that berm, like us, was protected.

The ditch we were crawling in was so shallow that we couldn't raise our heads and shoulders enough to talk to the man next in line. We kept contact by holding the foot of the man ahead of us. Sgt. Paul Bakos, crawling first, suddenly yelled, "Hey! There's a mine here." Hathaway, next in line, asked, "Where?" "Underneath me!" came the reply. "My God! Get off it!"

Bakos, after an anxious second, braced and slowly raised his body off the ground using his knees and elbows and crawled over the mine. That was how all of us made it. Keeping flush with the ground to avoid being hit by machine gun fire, we scraped over the circular top of the "Bouncing Betsy." We used our bayonets as walking sticks, much like that of a blind man, carefully scanning the dirt in front of us until we got out of that blasted area.

These mines, or "mustard pots" as we called them, were stationary explosive charges set off by contact with a moving object, such as someone stepping on the top of it. The explosion would take the foot and the leg and just splay it on out. Then shrapnel and parts of the casing would fly all over in maybe a thirty yard circle for the people on their feet close to it. These mines were nasty, real nasty. That's why we had to take our time. To discover the darn things it was just a matter of probing. They were probably spaced six to ten feet apart. When we did locate one, we used our bayonets as useful tools to disengage the deadly beasts, getting at the bottom of them.

While our progress was slowed greatly by the mine field, no mines were set off.

We stopped to rest in the cover of a thicket of scrub. We stayed here for three hours, dividing up two D bars and part of a canteen of water. None of us had eaten since landing. We even risked cigarettes, blowing the smoke into the ground.

After we had been there a couple of hours, Hathaway and I spotted a LCV coming in to the Pointe, two miles west. We used field glasses and could make out men getting into the LCV at the beach. The craft left the beach. Seeing no movement on the Pointe, we decided that the Pointe was being evacuated. We thought maybe the whole invasion had failed. This made us plenty scared.

We started off again west. Suddenly Sgt. Bakos just jumped up and hollered, "I'm going!" and ran off at a crouch. Bellows followed. No enemy fire came this time. The rest of us followed, spaced at long intervals.

We got back to the Pointe by following the cliff without further incident. We were relieved to find that the Pointe was not only occupied, but reinforced. I reported to Col. Rudder. Col. Rudder said, "You men look hungry. We have plenty of bread, jam, and spam. Go to it." We had not eaten for two days.

Super highway in
Germany Autobahn

Chapter Ten

The Days That Followed D-Day

*Morale is a powerful weapon, and the German
Army's morale is falling—fast.*

—Ace Parker

WE WERE THE only people there that fought in both places, on
Omaha Beach and at Pointe du Hoc. That was cited when I
got the Distinguished Service Cross.

It wasn't long afterwards when the remainder of the 5th and
2nd Battalions finally reached the Pointe on D+2. Also with
them were a Battalion of the 116th Infantry and tanks of the
743rd Tank Battalion, who were attacking Pointe du Hoc from
the southwest. They had been fighting for two whole days and
half of this one. There had been very little communication
between them and us on the Pointe. I think that when they got
there, they thought they were attacking the Germans. We were
aware this might happen. So we had taken an American flag,
placed it on a pole and flew it on top of one of the pillboxes.
When the tank got up there they shot the flag down and also
killed two 2nd Battalion Rangers and wounded six others.
There was a hell of a few minutes of panic trying to
communicate and shut things down. People were standing up
and frantically waving their hands and yelling.

When the 5th Rangers came into the Pointe on D+2, they
came in a rush! Jack Snyder, my friend, C Company
Commander, dove into a shell hole that I was crouched down
in. His helmet was down over his face from landing. He
pushed it up and looked at me and said, "Ace, you son of a
bitch! I thought you were dead." He owed me 300 dollars

from a poker game and jokingly pretended to be upset that I was still alive. I had been carried as missing in action. They didn't know where I and 23 of my company were. They didn't know if we were wounded; they didn't know if we were dead. So we were listed as missing in action. That news had spread like wild fire, particularly among the captains.

The Battalion regrouped, having its first chance to get together. Things had settled down. There was no sense of urgency. New leadership positions were assigned.

On the Pointe, the Germans had an awful lot of underground storage with interconnecting tunnels for shells and food. The Germans would pop up anyplace. They were very, very annoying. You'd see the dirt move aside and a German would pop up out of the bottom of a shell hole. It would be necessary to shoot him on the spot. So, you'd have to cover your back as this would be going on internally, inside the line. There were a couple of guys in our group that delighted in working the tunnels underground and flushing out the Germans that were down there. They were like rats. Sgt. William Kalar, a little overweight and a wild man, was one of them. He teamed up with a paratrooper that had fallen into the sea on D-Day and had been picked up on the way to the Pointe by the 5th Rangers. Kalar got a bullet in the neck, but it didn't tear his neck. He had enough loose skin. That was an awful lot of hot fight. It seemed wherever you were there was war.

The pillboxes on the Pointe had big openings much like a covered porch made out of concrete—steel reinforced cement. One could drive a truck in there and out the other side. The Germans would deliver supplies and ammunition here. I was standing in one of these openings with my back up against the pillbox and an artillery shell went through the alley whizzing by me. I could feel its wind as it went by. The shell came right down the middle, probably shot from a tank and probably one of ours. I just shrugged my shoulders. It was just one more thing that happened. I had the attitude that no one had gotten hurt—so forget it. Exciting days!

When we had gotten everything cleared up and organized, we hit the road, which would've been the beginning of day four. We were just behind Utah Beach, just east of the Pointe, and were headed towards Cherbourg. We were making a sweep inland, acting as the flank guard to an infantry unit, moving south of the road. Everybody was fighting their own battle here. We were not all walking down a highway in a line. We were spread out and knew that each of us may have to fight our own little war at a moment's notice. Even if others were only a hundred yards away they may not be able to help.

The Germans had built a strongpoint of batteries and a defensive complex of pillboxes here at Grand Camp Maisy. The Germans had chosen this particular site since from here they could see all the way down the coast. They had blown the dikes that had kept the sea water out. The dikes had been in place so that the French could farm the land. The Germans blew those dikes so that the enemy approaching from the sea or beach was slowed by the knee-deep swampy water. This is where our paratroopers had landed and explains why Utah Beach had less battle than Omaha Beach. The German troops were sucked off the cliffs and into the battle with the paratroopers. The Allies had also dropped paratrooper dummies. We ran across these as we walked. Parachutes were lying in the water, sometimes still attached to the man now dead. We also saw bodies hanging still harnessed in the trees — the paratrooper's chutes having caught here. There were piles of shells on the ground, 8 or 9 inches high, where Germans had stopped to fire at the paratroopers repeatedly.

This was not something we wanted to see. But nevertheless we took advantage of the situation and cut up the parachutes made of camouflage material, covering our helmets with the remnants. We then placed a net over the entire helmet. This broke the helmet's outline. The helmet is not a natural look. If spotted, the enemy can usually figure out that there is a man underneath it. We would stick brush and such into the netting to again camouflage it. We also used charcoal on our faces, especially on patrols. This would break up the contours of our faces. The whiteness of the skin could flash right out, alerting the enemy.

I'm pretty sure that I didn't have the same helmet all the way through. I might have just flat lost one. It would've been such an insignificant thing that I wouldn't have had any reason to remember it. It was a good idea, but very few guys got killed or badly wounded because they didn't have a helmet on. And anything below the eye line doesn't have coverage— doesn't have a helmet anyway. But if you were in the Third Army area the cover was up on the truck and your helmet was on your head. When Patton came in and took over in the area, new rules were enforced. You'd think that you could hold your helmet between your knees, riding along. But he wanted us to be able to fight even when we were being transported. Patton had a bunch of Provo marshals along the highway—cops. The MPs would pull the truck over and issue a ticket right there on the spot. The ticket would beat you back to headquarters.

The helmet was shaped round so bullets or shrapnel would glance off it. I think the Germans had the best looking ones. They came lower down on the head and probably served to protect the back of the neck more. The British helmets, however, were crazy. They were like shallow discs.

We, Companies A, C and F were assigned to advance down the road toward Maisy. The German pillboxes in this area were built like man holes—concrete fortresses underground. They had trenches that led into them and were built facing the sea. Now from here they could fire mortars. On the concrete wall in front of them they had marked the settings, the distances to places they wanted the shell to land, so they didn't have to guess. They had done this in the past, fired the shell and knew what it took to hit this spot or that spot. It was all there for them. They had been there for four years so they had lots of time to build up this thing.

At Maisy, we walked into the pill boxes from the trenches. We had to fight in the trenches. Generally, most of the fighting here was gun-to-gun combat. They gave up fairly rapidly. We were shouting at them and we had them coming out real good. They were putting down their weapons, putting their hands behind their heads and coming out. However, there were some SS officers in there who were screaming at their soldiers to continue to fight. They started shooting their own men in the back. Then, nobody dared to surrender. So we had to do the whole thing all over again. I came upon one officer, who was lying there dead, that I had to step across. He had held a hand grenade to the side of his head and blown the whole side of his head off in order not to surrender. He was an SS fanatic. It would have been a lot easier for both sides if those SS men had not been there—much fewer casualties would have occurred on both sides.

I imagine that the invasion disrupted everything for the Germans at Normandy, including payroll distribution. At Maisy, one man from C Company found their payroll in a suitcase. There it was, about 50,000 dollars in old French Francs, wrapped in nice packets. Everybody started grabbing it. Jack Snyder, one of my best friends, was the C Company Commander. It was his runner that I came upon, stuffing the money inside his fatigue jacket. I said, "Jeez, don't you know that stuff is no good? That's old Francs." He said, "Yeah, I know it and you know it, but the French don't know it. I'm going to use this to buy steaks and fresh eggs and real luxuries." Some of the guys were lighting their cigarettes with it. Some of them were using it for toilet paper.

For a month or more, if you got that stuff down to the beach, where the government now had set up a post office, you could buy a money order with it and send the money order home, so for awhile there was heavy traffic trying to get down to that beach. Then finally the government got smart. They said we could only send home what we had left out of our allotted pay. That's all we could send home and no more. That stopped thousands of it from being sent home in money orders.

I got a lot of it myself. I used it for poker. I was playing poker and craps and I was winning. We had a few "pigeons" that we just kept broke all the time. That means we plucked the money off them. George and I and Snyder were doing it. I got these extra winnings home by having the guys that weren't going to send anything home that month send my money home to their folks with instructions to send it to my folks. And nearly everybody did. So, when I came home I had a good $4000 in savings, which 55 years ago, was a lot of money.

That night, we assembled in a bivouac area west of Osmanville. The invasion operation was over. I remember that night as one of my squads asked me to join their circle because they had something they wanted to say to me. They had a fire going. They had been separated in battle shortly after landing on D-Day. The complaint was that the squad hadn't seen their squad mate for three days. (In civilian life this soldier had been a small tough Italian street fighter.) He claimed he was a prisoner. But they didn't believe him. They said they didn't want him around if they couldn't depend on him. So we transferred him. We transferred him to an infantry outfit that was presently fighting the Germans on the front line. You don't transfer someone to a nice cushy job someplace. So, he wasn't a Ranger anymore. We kicked him out. And all it took was a complaint by the whole squad. Without the confidence in each other we were weakened.

When we needed replacements we would go out and find somebody that wanted to volunteer. The "Repple Depple" (Replacement Depot) was a good place to find a replacement. The Replacement Depot was a sort of holding area at which men were waiting assignment to a unit. They might be just

Last pd by C.L. HATHAWAY, Major, F.D.

WAR DEPARTMENT
Form No. 336a—Revised
Form approved by Comptroller General, U.S.
September 23, 1940

D. O. Vou. No. _____

PAID BY

(For use of paying office)

WAR DEPARTMENT
PAY AND ALLOWANCE ACCOUNT
(Commissioned Officers, Army Nurses, Warrant Officers, Contract Surgeons)

APPROPRIATIONS :
PAY OF THE ARMY, 19____

212/50425 PSA 1942-45 60-114 P 411-01

(1) THE UNITED STATES, Dr.,
To CHARLES H. PARKER   Capt. Inf. (AUS) 0-1290298
(Name of payee)   (Rank and organization)

(2) Station APO 655, 5th Ranger Inf Bn   Station No._____
On duty at present station per Par_____, S. O. No. VOCO, Hdqrs. 3rd Army   8 Nov   19 44
Departed from _____ 19____ Reported for duty at _____ 19____

DEPENDENTS :

(3) Lawful wife : _____ or
(Seta her Christian or given name in full and husband's surname and her address each month)
Unmarried children under 21 years of age.

(State names, ages, and addresses each month. Evidence of dependency attached hereto or filed with voucher No.____
19____ accounts of.____)

(4) Dependent mother _____
(State her Christian or given name in full and husband's surname and her address each month)
During the current period for which allowances are claimed on account of my dependent mother I have contributed to her support
the sum of $_____, in cash or its equivalent, without any consideration in return, which contribution is her chief
support, and each and every statement set forth in her affidavit dated_____ 19____
(attached hereto), filed with voucher for the month of_____ 19____ is true and correct, and so
remains at this time, except _____
(State fully changes occurring between date of last affidavit and signing of this voucher)

(5) For over 3 years' service ; 3d pay period ; 3 years completed on   20 June   19 44

CREDITS   Amount

(6) For base and longevity pay from   1 Nov   , 144 , to   30 Nov   19 44
(7) For additional pay for Foreign Service from 1 Nov , 144 , to 30 Nov 19 44

(8) For pay for_____ amount_____ from_____ 19____ to_____ 19____
of which I was the actual and exclusive owner, which (was or were) suitable for the military service, and maintained
at _____
(9) For subsistence allowance from   1 Nov   , 1944 , to   30 Nov   19 44
(10) For rental allowance from_____ 19____ to_____ 19____
during which period I was not assigned adequate quarters at my permanent station ; if without dependents, I was
not on field or sea duty ; if with dependents, I did not occupy with any public quarters assigned to me without
charge at any station, nor did any of them occupy public quarters assigned to them or to any other officer or his
dependents, except for bona fide social visits

TOTAL CREDITS _____ $_____

DEBITS :   Amount

(11) Class XXXXXXXXXX Insurance Foreign "D" Almt $ 77 50
(12) Class "E" Allotment   160 00
(13) Class "N" National Service Life Insurance   6 50
(14) Due United States for 92 meals for Oct 1944 at 25¢   23 25

TOTAL DEBITS _____ $_____
NET BALANCE _____ $_____

(15) On____ (ordinary or sick) leave or absence ; Departed_____ 19____ under Par____ S. O. No.____
Hdqrs._____ 19____ ; extended by Par____ S. O. No.____ Hdqrs.____
_____ 19____ Returned_____ 19____

(16) I certify that the foregoing statement and account are true and correct ; that payment therefor has not been received ; and that payment
to me as stated on the within pay voucher is not prohibited by any provisions of law limiting the availability of the appropriation(s)
involved.
Place to my credit with_____
(SIGN
ORIGINAL
ONLY)

Date   30 Nov   44

MEMORANDUM
Capt. Inf. (AUS)

(17) I certify that during the period for which rental allowance is claimed on this voucher the above officer was not assigned adequate quarters at
his permanent station.
(SIGN ORIGINAL ONLY, ON   Name_____
MEMORANDUM, TYPE, OR   Rank_____
Date_____ 19____ PRINT NAME AND RANK)   Commanding Officer.

(18) Paid by { Check(s) No.(s)_____ dated_____ 19____ for $_____ (SIGN ORIGINAL ONLY)
{ Cash, $_____ on_____ 19____

for Treasurer of the United
States in favor of payee named
above.

MEMORANDUM

HQ 808

entering from a hospital in England or newly arrived from the U.S. Men picked from here had seen combat, had been wounded and were now healed ready for action. In the regular army, the men didn't have the privilege of going back to their same unit after leaving the "Repple Depple". Our people that had been wounded, treated and healed could not be sent to somebody else. They would come back to us. Then the guys were fighting with soldiers they knew, that they had trained with. These were special people—the men were.

We interviewed the replacements one-on-one. We chose someone that spoke with some resolve and intelligence. We screened him, trained him, and fed him back in. We had him around long enough so that everybody trusted him within the squad. A squad was only a few people. They had to learn to expect that certain basic things were going to be done. They needed to know that their squad member was not going to cower down, hide, or dig himself a bigger hole, that type of thing. The squad knew within themselves everybody's skill level also. If there were some things that one of the guys was particularly good at, they would defer to him on their own. And I might hear about it. The squad leader would tell the platoon leader and the platoon leader would tell the captain and well, you just knew where they were. Everybody was exceptional. But this was the exceptional of the exceptional.

Shortly after, awards were handed out. I was among the receivers.

CITATION FOR DISTINGUISHED-SERVICE CROSS

First Lieutenant Charles H. Parker, 01290298, Infantry, U. S. A. For extraordinary heroism in action on 6th, 7th, and 8th of June, 1944 from Vierville-sur Mer to Le Pointe du Hoc, France. In the invasion of France, Lieutenant Parker led his company up the beach against heavy enemy rifle, machine gun and artillery fire. Once past the beach he reorganized and continued inland. During this advance numerous groups of enemy resistance were encountered. Through his personal bravery and sound leadership this resistance was overcome, and his company succeeded in capturing Le Pointe du Hoc, the Battalion objective. The following morning Lieutenant Parker led a patrol through enemy territory in an effort to establish contact with the balance of the Battalion. Lieutenant Parker's valor and superior leadership are in keeping with the highest tradition's of the service. Entered Military service from South Dakota.

France, June 23

Dearest Mother, Dad and Carmen,
    I was decorated today with the second highest award the Government gives. A Lt. General pinned a "Distinguished Service Cross" on me this morning. Two of the men of my company were rewarded the same citation. I recommended them and a board of high officers passed it. My citation was recommended by my commanding officer, a Colonel.
    It was earned on the battlefield during some of the toughest fighting this war has seen. I never in the world had any idea I was going to get it and I'm quite sure I don't deserve it. This Battalion is the best bunch of men in the whole army. We came in on D-Day at "H" hour and made possible the beach head on the coast of France. In the midst of some very intense fighting we held our position for four days. The two Battalions of Rangers are receiving the "Presidential Unit Citation." In order to do that the unit has to do an act which would be the equivalent to

every individual earning a D.S.C. Some day
I'll tell you all about it. Charles

When my captain bars caught up with me out in the field, we had a little ceremony at which time someone pinned them on me. Everything would have been peaceful around us or we would not have had the ceremony. I wore them until it was not time to wear them anymore—until we went back into battle. Insignia of rank, anything that would tell a sniper what your rank was, was making yourself a target. A sniper was a very discerning man—he wasn't just trying to kill any soldier that came along. Usually they would try to target officers. And the salute, for heavens sake, one might as well wear a badge that says sergeant, or first sergeant, or an officer's bar! I told my guys that if they saluted me out in the field that I would shoot them myself. Another give-away as to my rank was that I usually would be around the big radio used to communicate back to battalion (Headquarters). They'd see that big antennae sticking up there and would know that was the headquarters of the outfit.

I had three medics. John Burke was a good-looking guy, baby-faced and young. He was our first medic. He got wounded and was gone. Then I got my second one. He was probably over educated for us. He admired the Rangers that had come through—no whining, stoic. So he volunteered to join us. They took him and I got him. Most of the medics that went with us had field training. He had just the shortest amount when he came to us. On the Cherbourg Peninsula I had the unit practice coming in on the beaches. I watched from above on the cliff. The mine field was there but we had it staked. I told him, "Stay behind. Don't come." But he just couldn't stand it and got curious. I went through. He followed me in. It only knocked me down but it blew his leg off.

Another incident with a mine I remember well. We were just sitting around. We were lickin' our wounds, trying to get

Colonel Max Schneider

Captain Charles Parker receiving
the Distinguished Service Cross

Left to right: Max Schneider, George P. Whittington, Charles H. Parker, Francis W. Dawson,
Willie Moody, Howard McKissick, Denzil R. Johnson, Alexander W. Barber

"It only remained to bury the dead and award the medals—and
when General Bradley paid a visit two weeks later for the latter
purpose, he was accompanied by General George S. Patton. While
they were waiting for the ceremony to begin, some of my friends
were close enough to hear Bradley say to Patton, "For Christ sake,
Georgie, suck in your gut."   —Stan Askin

washed, shaved and all this sort of thing. We weren't fighting anybody. We had been recruiting because we needed replacements. We had accepted some of them. And I got one, a first lieutenant, with a good Polish name, Wybroski. Aloysious Wybroski. He was going to be a goody. I was real happy about him. He was going to be a good platoon leader.

Most of our eggs were from powder—scrambled eggs. So, a chance to have a fresh egg, an actual fresh egg that you could poach or boil or fry, was a delicacy. We could see a farm a short distance away, half mile or so. We decided to get us some fresh eggs, but we had to cross a pasture with a fence around it. There were milk cows within the fence. There were no cows injured so it appeared that there were no mines in there. It looked peaceful and safe. So we climbed the fence. I took Wybroski with me. We were visiting along the way, happily talking with each other and getting more and more information—like the kind of people we were. Subconsciously I was making up my mind about this fella. Lord, all of a sudden he stepped on a mine and down he went. It had blown his foot off and shattered his bone up the shin quite a ways. He was a blocky, short man. I don't imagine he was over 5'8" and probably weighed close to 180 pounds. I couldn't carry him alone. I didn't know where the rest of the mines were, either. I decided to go for help. Well, I got out of there covering the ground where we had walked side by side. At that point I could cut loose and ran back to camp and there grabbed a bunch of guys.

Four of us took a jeep and went back to get Wybroski. The jeep waited for us on the other side of the fence. We didn't know where the thunder the mines were. It was a step at a time to see if we could detect any disturbance, any little evidence that there was anything under there. We got out of the mine field with him. Then we put him into the jeep and took off for Cherbourg. We were that close to Cherbourg. The port city of Cherbourg had by now been taken by the Allies. There was a big hospital set up there. I remember that journey—it was a paved road full of pot marks and holes and it was awfully hard not to hit them. Whenever we hit a hole, Wybroski would scream with the jar. We didn't dare give him much more morphine because he was going to get into this hospital and have surgery. We just tried to take the top off it.

As soon as we got there, the surgeons and the nurses operated on him right away. I remember the surgeons coming out of the surgery and telling us that they had to take his leg off below the knee. We hung around and waited until they got him out of surgery. I came back to see him in the days following. He went back to the United States, the Zone of the Interior. I never heard from him or of him again.

In one of our travels we came upon a small French village that was empty. We decided that this night we were going to sleep under cover. The gardens were good ones—vegetables and potatoes. And chickens. Of course the men immediately ran down a few chickens to cook us up a good stew. One particular house was small with a one car garage. To the side of the garage the hedgerows formed a head-high bank. We spread our bags and our blankets down in the garage. It was just an empty sheet-metal garage. There was probably about 5 or 6 of us in there, just the headquarters group. That would've been the Command Post. Wherever the Company Commander was, that was the Command Post.

Pfc. Ralph Boyer, Tec 5 Jesse Tayler (the radio man), the first sergeant (the platoon sergeants would have been out with the platoons), and a runner, probably Frank McGuire, would have been in there. And we were bone tired. We never got enough good sleep, so it was always a dead sleep. We depended on the people on guard to alert us. So, we're in there sleeping, lying fairly closely grouped, when just for no reason whatsoever, I awakened. There wasn't a sound or anything else—I wasn't due to get up and check and see what was going on. I just woke up in an absolute total panic. I shouted at everybody, "Get up and go. Leave things the way they are. Just go, get out! Get across the road and against the wall."

The wall was an embankment. And boy, we had just barely gotten there when two shells came in and just blew the garage all apart. The Germans were constantly probing with their artillery, because by this time they knew that we were there. The men looked with big eyes at each other. That was one close call.

You get a lot of hunches. But they're good hunches most of the time based on even subliminal observations. But this just came totally out of the blue. I imagine that was the only true extra-sensory experience that I ever had. I always thought of it as that. I couldn't blame intuition or anything for it. We were sleeping hard. The guards were all posted. Shifts were all set up. There was no reason to be on alert.

August 8, 1944, France

Dearest Folks,
    Everyone hopes for an early end to this struggle and nearly everyone thinks we should see its end soon. I mostly hope that everyone else is right. We are all watching closely the situation on Hitler's home front for morale is a powerful weapon and the German Armies morale is falling. Fast. All my love, Charles.

I remember another incident very well since it involved a beautiful woman. We were in an apple orchard. Here there was a river and a waterfall. We didn't have any showers. The large units did and the permanent ones—the hospitals, the cooks, and that sort of thing. It didn't make any difference if we were whiskered. We'd shave when we didn't have anything else to do. Then we would shave and wash and brush our teeth. We washed ourselves as best we could. Sometimes

we would heat some water in a helmet and take a swab down. We'd build a little fire. When the coals got low, we'd heat our water in the helmet. We could go weeks before we had a chance to brush our teeth. Maybe we lost our tooth brush. As a result, often times they would put little things like that in with food rations. They might add a little box of cigarettes, a tooth brush or toothpaste. They knew that we might have lost the darn thing or that we might have used it for something else.

So the edict went out, "Everyone will get under the waterfall and bathe. We will get some clean clothes for you." Soap was issued to everybody. There are pictures of all of us under that waterfall getting clean. I hated cold water all my life. I was full weight then. But I dreaded the thought of going into that damned river! Everybody else was going in but I figured, I'll skip this thing. I'll stand under that waterfall just long enough to get wet, get soap on and get it off. The guys thought to hell with that. So they threw me in the river. We heard that the USO, a huge organization, was putting on shows with young women, dancers and such. Bob Hope was the host and the group was going all over the European theater to entertain the troops. The performers were out there without their big salaries but got their payoff in the adulation that the soldiers gave them. They had a part in the war. And by gosh, there was to be a show fairly close to us! Dinah Shore was the featured person on it. So we were getting cleaned up and ready to go to this show

Then we got a sudden call. There was a mission for us and we had to leave right away. Somebody told the USO people that the Rangers had gotten a call to leave and wouldn't be at the show. When Dinah Shore's group found out they decided to come out to us. We were tearing down tents, packing up things and here's Dinah Shore. She was walking along the hedgerows in her fatigues singing to the men a cappella as they packed up. The men told her stories about how much I liked her singing and how beautiful I thought she was. Then they led her to me. She came right up, right in front of my face. I think the song that she sang was *"How Come You Do Me Like You Do... Do... Do."* And I stood there entranced. The other guys were around us. After that song, she sat on the hood of a jeep and sang some more as the troops gathered around. You never had such an enthusiastic audience. Then we left. So I never really saw a USO show.

Behind the lines, our American troops sang on a regular basis. A truckload of soldiers would pass another and one could hear them singing at the tops of their voices, "Roll me over in the clover...Roll me over....and do it again." The whole truckload would be roaring. Verses would vary and be thought of on the spot. There was a lot of that. As trucks passed each other the other truck would, in good nature, boo. The big thing about it was that American soldiers didn't just sit in the trucks. You didn't hear singing from the British or the French. Only the Americans showed that much spontaneity and enthusiasm.

We always tried to keep our feet clean. I was constantly reminding the men to take care of their feet because that was our major means of transportation. The feet were always a problem for an infantryman. Whenever we were marching long distances, we would take a five or ten minute break every hour. I never really got a chance to sit down myself as I would be moving up and down the column checking on everybody's feet. The men would flop down on the side of the road. It was a good time to take the shoes off and air the feet out a little bit. Get the toes moving. Maybe somebody noticed a little discomfort. Maybe there was a wrinkle in the sock. He would take the shoe off and examine the foot. If a foot infection were to get bad enough, then that person would be practically useless. We would lose a man.

The socks were an army green, a tannish-green and made of wool. They generally came to just below the knee. We washed our own socks. We always made room someplace in our packs for extra socks.

I never had any trouble with my feet. I had blisters but I never had anything that stopped me. If we were going a lot on foot, and the situation was such that we couldn't lay back, relax and take off our shoes and socks, a person's feet could get awfully tender. But if we were walking all the time, walking, walking, walking, a person would get like a kid in the summertime that goes barefoot. He could go across gravel and driveways and everything else at the end of the summer. But at first he couldn't. If the boot didn't have exactly the right fit, which it seldom did, our foot would be allowed to slide a little when we stepped. The heel would come forward or slide too far back. Then we would get this rubbed raw area. Our feet were always a matter of concern.

The *Stars and Stripes* was the newspaper for the military. There was a different edition for each theater of the war—one for the South Pacific, one for Africa and Italy, and one for Europe. Bill Mauldin was with the press corps and wrote for the Stars and Stripes. Mauldin was moved over to Europe from Africa. That's where he became well known as a cartoonist. He was extremely famous amongst the troops. Mauldin's cartoons of Willie and Joe, his two characters, were soldiers that specifically were infantry men. Boy, I'll tell you, that was a clean shot of life as it was. Those two soldiers were absolutely worn out. One cartoon that I remember is of Willie and Joe marching down the line with a whole bunch of other guys, bearded and bent over, shuffling along. One of them has got a condom at the top of his rifle. The caption underneath read, "It keeps the rifle and the inner works dry." And so everybody immediately started using them for that purpose. Bill Mauldin's stuff was something else. He came back here and was a cartoonist for a major paper in Chicago for a long time.

Condoms had another purpose. We used them to blouse out

our pants at the bottom. Pants have a tendency to pull up when you sit or move about. We tied a condom at the bottom and then bloused the pant out over the boot. They worked good because they didn't break. This also provided a seal at the top of the boot so no sticks or stones could get inside the boot. In the case of the Ranger, we had parachute boots that stood 10 inches tall and were laced tightly around the ankle and up. The paratroopers were the first to get this type of boot as they wanted a boot that would stay on through the jump and survive their roll in the landing.

It rained a lot. Perhaps that's all the smoke that goes up to form rain drops or perhaps the noise creates rain. But, it seems to me that wherever you find a war going on, you find mud.

I wrote home on October 24, 1944:

> The weather is very dreary—rains all the time and mud to the eyebrows is the fashion. However, our position could and has been so much worse that I can't complain about anything.

We sloshed our way through the blasted mud. It rained and rained and rained. It loused things up for everybody. It kept the airplanes out of the air so they couldn't support us. It stalled the ground transportation. It made it miserable for the troops that had to walk. It was miserable. We had no coverings for the boots. Just boots. But we had raincoats. Some of the raincoats would be cape-like things. That was a guarantee that everything below the rim was going to be sopping wet because the rain would run off that thing. The raincoats weren't generally on us. They often would be back in the supply truck. So if it was initially just starting to rain then we were going to get wet. If we were wet at night, then we were going to be miserable. There would be a chill. We would then have a devil of a job trying to keep our weapons clean. But rolled up in our sleeping bag we usually had a change of clothing.

We used purifying pills so that we could drink the water out of the streams and rivers. These were chlorine tablets. Europe generally wasn't a problem for water but Asia was another story. We also drank wine whenever it was available.

The cigarette lighter that we carried to light our cigarettes was called a Zippo. The government contracted with a number of tobacco companies to supply cigarettes to the troops. Whichever cigarettes came up that week, we got in our rations. The cigarettes back then were shorter because they had no filter. Lucky Strike made a slogan out of the fact that they changed their packaging from the green color they had been using, which required a derivative of copper, to white. All the metal went to the war effort. Then they created a new slogan, "Lucky Strike Goes to War." Cigarettes became an item of commodity. The guys that didn't smoke were very popular— everyone vying to get their cigarettes.

The transportation unit over there was called the "red ball," which hauled goods all over. They would haul ammunition, food, and just everything out of the ports. They formed up large convoys. The thing would be high-balling along. An officer would be positioned at the front and another officer at the back in jeeps and they would run along on the sides. As they would be going through the city, it wouldn't be unusual for one of these transportation drivers to take the truck at an intersection and drive it off to a side street and sell the whole darn thing. Then they would live in the city off the profits. So the MPs were constantly on the lookout for these deserters that had left with a truck.

We had no transportation of our own as part of our deal. I think we had one 2 ½ ton truck and a couple of jeeps that were the 5th Battalion's. But the company commanders had none.

Sullivan told us if we wanted transportation, go out and get it. That meant—steal it. So we ended up with every company commander having a jeep. We got in trouble, though. A couple of goof balls in the company had stolen an old MP jeep, outfitted with all the flashing lights and everything. They stripped all those out but now were left with holes in the fender where the lights used to be. Any MP that's looking for some of these stolen jeeps knew this was an MP jeep immediately. It had to be hurriedly gotten rid of. We put it back in the woods to hide it. It was just too "hot."

On guard in the trenches, there weren't any subjects that were off limits. We talked. It depended upon the mood, the danger, and everything else. Sitting on those lonely vigils, when we weren't grabbing every moment we could to sleep, we talked about everything that occurred to us—about parents and home life, plans and dreams. We knew by this time that we were going to have a little money. We'd been sending some home. Also, the GI Bill was available. The GI Bill would pay for our college tuition and living expenses.

I wasn't sure what I wanted to be. All my life I kind of wanted to be a forester. I loved the woods. We didn't have a lot of woods where I grew up but we had the river a couple of miles from town. That was always a little wooded. Then, when I went into the CCC out in the Black Hills, I became really interested in forestry.

We were issued morphine syrettes to relieve pain as needed. Everybody had his own packet with sulfa and tape. So, the medic most of the time, could use the packet of the guy that was hurt. Sulfa was an antibiotic with limited coverage. It was particularly good against gram negative organisms like with urinary infections. Penicillin came along in 1943 and that was a big help to the the aid man. Penicillin was given in a place that had a lot of tissue—like the upper shoulder or the fanny. It was very crude. I was put on penicillin for four or five days when I had pneumonia. It was suspended in peanut oil. When

I got it in the hip, it felt like that if I moved my toes they would shatter like glass. The darn peanut oil really straightened that leg out.

I liked to carry one of the M-1s. That's a rifle that weighs between eight and nine pounds. You have to have a bunch of clips for it. A clip holds maybe eight bullets. So, if you empty a clip, a metal thing that is reusable, you can load it back up again. Then the Army put out a carbine. We didn't have them when we first went into the war, but later on we did. It was a light gun that shot a lighter shell. I had no faith in the carbine. So I carried my M-1. It wasn't part of my TO (Table of Organization), however. My gun, as an officer, was a 45 pistol worn on the hip for personal use and a Thompson submachine gun, 45 caliber. I carried a Thompson until it got smashed. A piece of shrapnel hit the receiver area which is the working area where the ammunition comes up. Then I picked up the M-1. I had a lot of faith in the M-1.

A letter to my sister:

France July 20, 1944

Dearest Muriel, Ed, and all,
    Well, nothing much doing now days…for me. I'm just sort of drifting along, taking it easy and being happy about it all. If I don't quit this good eating I'll gain a few ounces. I'm so skinny, you know, that I can turn sideways to the enemy and disappear. Handy little trick at times.
    My company is lying around under the trees with me toying with German weapons, writing letters home and generally being lazy.
    Last night the Sgt. of the guard woke me up "cause he smelled something sweet in the area." It was about 2:30 in the morning. So I

stumbled around with him, falling in fox
holes, bumping into trees and scratching my
legs up. We arrived at the area where the
odor was prevalent and started to
investigate. In a few minutes I found the
answer. One of the lads had used sweet
smelling bath powder for foot powder and the
Sgt. thought it was gas. There is always
something to keep things moving.

A little earlier that same night, I was
sleeping, when all of a sudden I heard one of
the guards shout and shoot. "Goddam it! Put
that–" Bang!! "–light out!" Bang!!! I don't
know who was scared most–the boy lighting the
cigarette–the guard, when I roared at him–or
me.

Yap! Never a dull moment.

On D Day I got a D.S.C. that is the second
highest award in the army–I don't know how it
could happen to me. Besides that the whole
Battalion got the Presidential Citation for
unit.

It's a great life for those who like it.
As for me, I'll take that "little ole vine
covered cottage" or sumpin.

When the world quits biting itself in the
back, I'd like to spend some time with you
doing nothing except just nothing.

Wine and champagne are good over here and
the girls are quite friendly. There are some
Germans here who don't like us very much. I
think they are going home soon though.

Tell Jackie and Billie that I'll be out to
play them a game of marbles next summer.
Maybe we can go for a horse back ride.

Say hello to Gerda for me next time you
write and be good–be happy and have fun too,
will you. All my love, Charles.

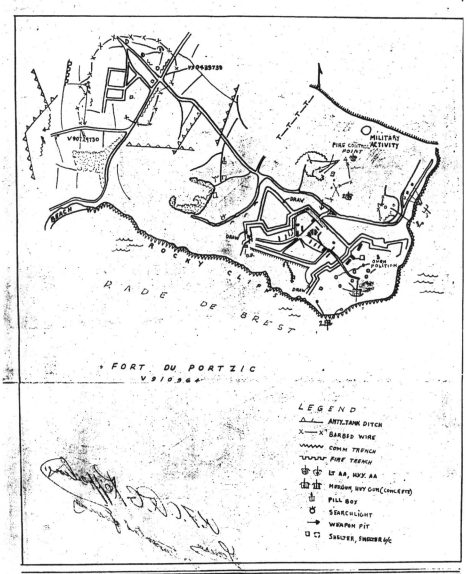

V9042975?

V9072973O

MILITARY ACTIVITY

FIRE CONTROL POINT

BEACH

DRAW

DRAW

OWN POSITION

ROCKY CLIFFS

DRAW

RADE DE BREST

FORT DU PORTZIC
V910964

LEGEND

△▲△	ANTI-TANK DITCH
x — xˢ	BARBED WIRE
∿∿∿	COMM TRENCH
⊔⊔⊔⊔	FIRE TRENCH
⊕ ⊕	LT AA, HVY. AA
⊞ ⊞	MEDGUN, HVY GUN (CONCRETE)
⊔	PILL BOX
♨	SEARCHLIGHT
→	WEAPON PIT
▫ ▭	SHELTER, SHELTER 4/c

OCCUPIED 18 SEPTEMBER 1944 BY 5ᵀᴴ RANGER BN. AND 1ˢᵀ BN. 115ᵀᴴ INF. AFTER SURRENDER OF ENEMY
FORCES WEST OF PENFELD RIVER

Chapter Eleven

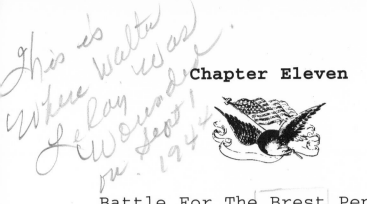

Battle For The Brest Peninsula

It was awful lonely out there around one of those pillboxes.

—Ace Parker

THE BATTLE FOR Brest, France, was one of the longest, most difficult and costly campaigns of the war for the Rangers. Brest, a peninsula, was the second largest port in France and contained some 80,000 people. It had been the principle submarine base for the German navy. The Allies needed the ports to carry the logistical flood of men and materials pouring into Europe. Cherbourg was very important for that reason also.

Brest had been bypassed in earlier attacks and the German defenders had become isolated.

Here at Brest the Germans had pens for their submarines. They would run them in undercover, close the top and nobody would know they were there. The Germans could furnish them, refurbish them, repair them—the whole bit. Then off they went on another mission. Brest was very important to the Germans for this reason.

The Allies were able to get stuff off the beach now at Omaha and Utah. But a port city, where you could bring your ships, tanks and everything else up close, was ideal. Brest was just down the coast from Omaha and Utah.

Brest was a network of forts and pillboxes—a city so well fortified that the Germans considered it unconquerable. Though we were a small unit, we played a role many times our size in the capture of the port.

The Battle for the Brest Peninsula campaign began for us Rangers on August 29, 1944. Virtually nothing has been published about it. General Troy Middelton's VIII Corps had the mission of capturing Brest. An order from their general attached two of our Ranger companies, A and C, to the Second U.S. Division. We were to relieve a company of the 23rd Infantry. A company in the regular army is a lot larger than one of our companies.

We took up position overlooking Pyrotechnic De St. Nicholas, securing the left flank of the 23rd and protecting the Guipovas-Brest Road. Intelligence thought it was 20,000 Germans that were entrenched at Brest, but the actual number was closer to 50,000—about the same size as the American force present at Brest. There was one fort after another in Brest, and they were trickier than hell. The Germans would take hay and cover an entire pillbox with it. We would think it was a haystack—until we saw the smoke and gunfire coming out of the thing. We never knew which direction the fire was going to come from.

I had a staff sergeant named Wilbur Ingalls. In a recent conversation he recounted an incident that happened at Brest. This is his memory:

> "One day we crossed quite a big field. I remember coming up out of a valley. Ace was getting his men lined up because we were going to charge across this 25 to 30 acre field. There was a tank trap in the middle of it. A tank trap would be a big ditch—dug and camouflaged—so the enemy tank would sink. We could see the ditch out there. Let me tell you how Ace operated. He got his men together—like Clyde Farrell—one of his sergeants. I was in Clyde's section. Ace said, 'You're going to be here on the left and you're going to be here on the right.' There was a haystack there and part of an infantry division. They

had a heavy machine gun under a haystack. The minute we showed ourselves we would begin to get long range fire from the fort and the pillboxes with machine gun fire. I can remember Ace asking the infantry guys, 'Will you fire on the machine guns to give us some cover—to help draw fire?' And they wouldn't do it! They felt that they might give away their position. Ace said, 'All right. Then we're going anyway!' So we took off running. Well, when we hit the tank trap ditch, there were Germans in there. The fifteen to twenty Germans surrendered with their hands up. We ran them up out of the ditch and made them run ahead of us with their hands up. And of course that stopped the machine gun fire.

"Then we got across the field and into the hedgerows. Now we were close to the pillboxes that were outside the fort. We held our position during the night. We were out in the open behind the hedgerows, hedgerows similar to those of the Normandy terrain. The hedgerows were made out of dirt and about four to five feet high. We heard noises but we didn't know what they were. Down under us the Germans had dug trenches. It turned out that my BAR man was close to the pillbox hole. He spotted it. In the morning we got about 45 Germans out from underneath us that were dug in and hiding there. We got them out by telling them to get out or we would get a grenade and throw it in there if they didn't."

The forts were larger pillboxes. They were located at the center with a series of smaller pillboxes built around them. People flowed in and out of those things by way of trenches. They were stocked with a depository of ammunition and food in case they got cut off from the normal supply route.

While at Brest, Col. Rudder had nominated Lt.Edlin of the

2nd Rangers, to take a reconnaissance patrol, locate the mine fields, and bag a prisoner or two for intelligence. This is his story. It's hard to believe, but it's true.

"Early in the morning on September 10th, we came to within two hundred yards of one of the largest pillboxes I had ever seen. The fort itself stood before us as tall as a ten story building. We were so close that their 88s or mortars could not fire on us. Only their machine guns and rifles could get us.

"We ran into a patrol from the 5th Rangers, led by Lt. Parker. We were good friends but still competitive. He told me he had the same mission as I, to locate the minefields so the 5th Rangers could move in. I told him they weren't going to beat us there. He replied, "Hell, I'll just take over the whole fort." I answered, "I don't think so. We'll take it over first." We were both joking.

"Lt. Parker moved ahead to chart the minefields. At a high stone wall I told my platoon sergeant, William Klaus, to hold the rest of the platoon there and cover us. Sgt. Bill Courtney, Sgt. Bill Dreher, and my runner, Warren Burmaster, and I moved to within fifteen or twenty yards of the pillbox. The minefield ahead of us was posted, but there were no signs telling us the path through it.

"Bill Courtney suddenly said, 'I see a way through the mines.' He started forward. We followed him. We could now see an obvious path, probably used by French civilians to bring in supplies.

"We went to the mouth of the pillbox. The doorway was open and we could hear Germans talking inside. I motioned to Burmaster to cover us. He was an excellent man and would report back to the company if something happened to us. We entered the pillbox.

We must have surprised them as we met no resistance. We learned that they had no idea any of us were within several miles. We captured the emplacement containing thirty-five men or so and took over their machine guns. We commandeered their radio equipment before they could use it. There was no firefight whatsoever.

"There I was, twenty-two years old, sitting with prisoners in the shadow of one of the strongest emplacements on the peninsula. I called in Burmaster and told him to have the radioman back with the rest of the platoon notify Col. Rudder and Capt. Arman that we had captured the pillbox and were within two hundred yards of the fort itself.

"I knew if I asked Col. Rudder if we should go ahead and try to enter the fort he would likely say no. He would say it was just too much of a risk. But if I waited for permission and didn't get it, there would be an all-out assault and a lot of men would be killed. There were only four of us and we had a chance to prevent this.

"I decided to go into the fort. Courtney had been speaking to one of the captured lieutenants who spoke fluent English. He said he could take us directly in to the fort and up to the fort commander. I left Dreher and Burmaster to stay with the prisoners and to notify Rudder that Courtney and I had gone to the fort. They were to hold all firing until they heard from Burmaster. Courtney spoke pretty good high school German and this might come in handy.

"The German lieutenant guided us through a minefield and to the entrance of the fort. We came down through a tunnel like in a football stadium, and when we opened the door, the German was in front and I was directly behind him, holding a Tommy gun in his back. We walked into a hospital room, the site of a large ward. There was an operating room in it and a lot of motion, white-clad doctors, nurses, and patients everywhere. When we showed up in American uniforms with guns in our hands it was just turmoil.

"Courtney, in his best German, yelled, *'Hande hoch!'* All hands went in the air. The German lieutenant asked if he could speak to them in German, and I agreed as long as he spoke slowly enough for Courtney to translate. Courtney heard him tell the Germans to remain calm, to sit down. He would lead us to the battery commander to try to negotiate a surrender and avoid more casualties.

"Everybody quietly went about their business, and we passed through the hospital section, the German in front, my gun in his back and Courtney behind me. The lieutenant would speak to several German soldiers on guard at the corridors. They immediately lowered their weapons. Courtney explained to me he was telling them I was being taken to their commander and not to cause problems or trouble.

"We came to a door and our German guide started to open it. I stopped him when he told Courtney it was the commander's office, LTC. Huerst. I instructed him to move aside. I turned the knob and stepped into the office with Courtney right behind me, our Tommy guns at the ready. A middle-aged colonel sat behind a large ornate desk. The room appeared like a modern office of today with carpet and everything. He was apparently surprised that anyone would enter without knocking. I immediately repeated Courtney's phrase, 'Hande hoch.'

"He raised his hands, and we closed the door behind us. I told Courtney to talk to him in German, but he answered that wouldn't be necessary. He spoke

English well. He seemed surprised at our presence. I told him that the fort was completely surrounded by American soldiers. We had already asked the air force and artillery to lift fire to give him a chance to surrender. I instructed him to immediately go on his PA system and announce that the whole fort should give up.

"He reached for his telephone. I said, 'Leave it alone.'

"'I just want to check to see how many Americans are really here,' he answered. I was in a tough position. About the only alternative I had was to shoot him, and that would gain nothing. So I let him call. He asked if we would care to have a drink. I couldn't have taken a drink—my stomach was upset, my heart was up in my throat. It's hard to say who was the most afraid, me or Courtney. We were in a position we couldn't back out of. If the German LTC surrendered, we'd have done a great job. If he didn't, then we obviously would become his prisoners. The two of us with Tommy guns could hardly defeat the whole garrison.

"The phone rang after a couple of minutes. He spoke in German. I looked at Courtney and he shook his head. The officer hung up and said, 'You are now our prisoners. There are only four Americans, two at the pillbox and you two.'

"For half a minute Courtney and I were prisoners, but we were very dangerous ones. I had decided that we would shoot him, barricade the office with desks, and wait until either the Germans got us or our guys attacked the next day, and when they came in, we'd still be alive.

"An idea struck my mind. I don't know where the idea came from or why I did it. I told Courtney to give me a hand grenade. Why I didn't use a knife or a

Tommy gun, I don't know. I took the grenade, pulled the pin, walked around the desk, and shoved it into the colonel's stomach. I told him to surrender or he was going to die right there.

"He said, 'You are bluffing. You'll kill all three of us.' I said, 'I'll show you how much I am bluffing. I'll count to three and turn loose the lever.' That would not be a pretty sight. It would flip off and the grenade would splatter his stomach and backbone all over the wall. He just sat there. I counted, 'One, two,' and he said 'All right, all right. I believe you.'

"I told him to get on the phone, use the PA system to announce to his men he had surrendered the fort, given up, and the combat was over. We would immediately get word to our battalion commander and stop any action coming in.

"He then asked me if he could tell his men that he had surrendered to a higher ranking officer than a Lt. in order to save face. I told him I didn't give a rat's ass who he said he surrendered to. I said I'd take him to my battalion commander and he could handle it.

"Over the PA system he spoke in German. Courtney understood him, and it was plain and clear that he had ordered his people to lower their arms and not take any hostile action against the American forces.

"I informed Rudder by radio what had happened. The Ranger CO confirmed he had notified the 29th Division commander and the 8th Corps commander of the surrender and there would be no artillery or air action. I was watching out the window for the surrender to begin. I wanted to make sure that this wasn't some kind of trap. The Germans started to file out. The sight was unbelievable. There were 850 people coming out. I had figured maybe 150 or even

250. It turns out that this particular fort was nine stories, two stories above ground and seven below. The commanding officer's office was on the top floor with windows. The German soldiers began stacking their arms in military fashion. This meant they disabled their own weapons and slipped the round lug bolt at the top of the barrel over the next weapon's barrel until a series of guns were stacked in a teepee formation.

"While we were inside Courtney was thinking that maybe we could get the German LTC to call General Ramke, the Brest commander, to surrender Brest completely. The LTC did call Ramke, but the General told him he didn't care if Huerst surrendered—he wasn't giving up yet. The bitter fight continued for another ten days.

"During the surrender ceremony, documents were formally signed and the commanding officer was supposed to give up his weapons. LTC Huerst reached down to draw his pistol but he had already given it up to me. They had to stop the ceremony, find me, retrieve the pistol and then continue on with the ceremony. After the ceremony Rudder asked me if I wanted the LTC's pistol. I told him that the Rangers were collecting a lot of pistols that day. No, I didn't need it. So Rudder held on to it. In 1965, when Rudder was on his death bed, one of the last things he said to his wife was, 'Contact Edlin and give him that pistol, because he deserves it.' Well, when his wife called me, she said if I didn't want it, it would be donated to the World War II museum in Grand Camp, France. I told her to go ahead and donate it to the museum. When I returned to Normandy for the 55th anniversary of D-Day in June of 1999, I had the opportunity to go to the museum. There it was, the LTC's pistol in a glass case with the inscription below, 'Donated By Colonel

Rudder and Lt. Edlin.' That was a thrill!

"After the ceremony, as we started to march off the prisoners, Col. Rudder congratulated the four of us and told us we had done a wonderful job. Then he called me aside and proceeded to tear me a new butthole. He was nearly crying considering the tremendous risk we had taken. I asked him what he would have done. Rudder answered he hoped he would have done the same."

Edlin's story reminded me of an experience that happened to me at Brest. I remember a narrow finger of land with water all around it on three sides. Across the water stood a massive fort that Sullivan wanted us to take. The only approach to it on the landward side from where we were was a railroad bridge. It had gotten to the point that just A and F Companies were there. Sullivan was back inland with the rest of the Battalion. He had been working to get rubber boats for us to attack across the water. I was worried about getting on those boats and going across that open water and then attacking the impenetrable fort. Looking across that blasted water scared the thunder out of us. First of all, there was no indication that the Germans were ready to yield. Second of all, previous to this we had been using anti-tank rockets that had merely bounced off the cement fort.

Col. Sullivan called in some P47's, fighter planes, and they dropped bombs on it. All of a sudden, right after the bombing, we looked across and saw the Germans flying some white flags out of the apertures of the fort. I decided to take them up on their offer. Me and my runner, Mac, walked across the railroad bridge totally exposed, and went in. Approximately two companies of men were lined up in formation all ready to surrender. They handed us the morning report with all their names listed on a roster. They were all ready to go. We counted to see if they were all there. The German officers even

"Ace"
I never knew his full name when I gave him my first Ranger salute;
But I could tell by his return salute that he knew his own resolute;
From then on we called him Ace Parker a fitting name for sure;
He took us to the gates of hell and back in a war that knew no cure;
He is in my prayers every night along with all the Rangers who fought and died;

I thank the Lord he was our leader in the battles we have fought side by side;
There is no other word to describe the man but Ace;
My Company Commander
Ranger Joe Drodwill

This card is an authentic reproduction of the official U.S. Army Christmas Card of 1944, which was given to troops in Europe to send home to family and friends.

helped Mac and I count. Then away we went marching off. The Battalion got there later. I also got chewed out for exposing myself and Mac to such danger.

It was awful lonely out there around one of those pillboxes. We were out there hammering at the door with a shaped charge trying to blow holes in the thing. The Germans, well protected under four feet of concrete in their pillboxes, were pouring everything they had into our troops that were attacking on foot. The gun of the pillbox was on the inside and was the only thing sticking out. And generally the pillboxes were rounded so that artillery would simply slide off. After a while, that got pretty doggoned disgusting.

We could only crawl so close to the pillbox because the area right around it was always bare. Both sides, during daylight hours, just kept shooting at each other. A few of us decided there's got to be a better way. So, I think it was George and I, that came up with the idea to take a five gallon can of gasoline, pour some of it out and put motor oil in it. Then we planned to pour that stuff down the air intake and put a shape charge on it and blow it. The air intake was a camouflaged vent on the side of the pillbox used to suck the air in and exhaust it someplace else quietly.

Well, George and D Company were given the job to do it. So, George went back and told his company what they were going to do. The job required that the patrol be very, very quiet—any clinking, any noise, even the slightest sound, would alert the Germans immediately.

By this time we had been bellied up against the pillboxes long enough to figure out where the air intake was going to be. So, he assigned the thing to Lt. Dawson. Lt. Frank Dawson announced the plan to his platoon. He called for volunteers. Well now, everybody is a volunteer! Dawson was asking for volunteers amongst volunteers! The guys were thinking, "This is mission impossible. There's no damn way I'm going to do that!" And nobody volunteered.

George was so mad—and he stayed that way—because he lost the job. His men, D Company, didn't get it done. So, they gave it to E Company. Jimmy Green, a West Point graduate and Commander of E Company, found a few men. He only needed enough to carry the cans and the beehive—the shaped charge. This was the explosive. It came down like a V and met a thousand of them all the way around the circle—all pointing for the diminishing point. When it exploded it would go around the inside of the pillbox like a hive of bees and shatter it all. So, they took a 5 gallon can of oil and gasoline mix, poured it down the air intake, stuck the shaped charge in the intake, pulled the fuse and ran. There was a timer on it, and they counted the seconds remaining as they ran. They threw themselves on the ground when they heard it go off. And when it went off it was awesome!

The rest of us Rangers waited and watched. We had stopped firing when the patrol reached the pillbox. The explosion came at around 10:00 PM and lit the sky for forty minutes. Every man on the patrol returned safely. Next morning, 18 September, 1944 the Germans surrendered. The Brest Battle was over. We inspected the pillbox Captain Green's patrol had blown. The box had been thoroughly destroyed, and the bodies of seventeen Germans were found inside. The prisoners taken from adjacent installations stated that the effect of the explosion had so defeated their spirits that many had remained awake and on alert all night. They lost their nerve. They believed we had used special ammunition, something like a flame thrower.

Who knows how long the battle at Brest would have taken if this hadn't happened. This certainly created its end or contributed to it. In spite of the good outcome, I don't think Battalion Headquarters would have asked that same bunch to do it again because of the extreme danger.

We gathered up everybody ahead of us and proceeded to the docks and the submarine tanks. These were on the edge of the city at the water's edge. The submarine pens were all under big rock—massive tunnels that had been dug back.

One of the Germans escorted me down into a Commidante's office. There the Commidante formally handed me his Luger. He then invited me to have a glass of wine with him, which I did. In English he stated, "The battle is over you say. If you're willing to be civilized, well so am I!" We sat down at a little table in one of his underground rooms. Most of the guys would have done the same thing. I don't imagine that he was in charge of the whole German force on the Brest Peninsula. It was my impression that he was a German paratrooper and a high ranking officer. I believe it was his paratroop division that wiped out the Rangers at Cisterne down in Italy. I was very happy we were able to take Brest. All of us were.

When I was down in the submarine pens, I came upon some leather coats hanging on a rack along one of the hallways. The leather coats were worn by the German officers. They were black and came all the way down to their ankles. I found one that fit me and I took it. I carried that coat around for about a month. It was quite heavy, solid leather. There was just no way I was going to carry that contraption around anymore, so I left it someplace. For awhile, I had a submarine man's coat!

At the end of this battle, the Free French added a little humor by pretending to be conquering soldiers. They pulled their guns, snatched uniforms out of a closet someplace and put them on. They marched through the city of Brest to music, make-believing that they had been part of the battle and victory. The French loved it and cheered enthusiastically.

In the Battle of Brest, we Rangers had captured 2,114 prisoners, killed 624 enemy and suffered 137 Ranger casualties.

HEADQUARTERS, 29TH INFANTRY DIVISION
A.   P. O. NO. 29, U. S. ARMY

"29 LET'S GO"

18 September 1944
SUBJECT: Commendation

TO: Commanding Officer, 5th Ranger Battalion.
(THRU: Commanding General, VII Corps)

1.   I desire to commend you and the members of
your Battalion for superior participation in active
combat while attached to this division during the
period 1-18 September 1944, culminating in the
capture of the City of Brest.
2.   Without exception, your Battalion has taken all
of its objectives quickly and with minimum losses.
Throughout your cooperation and enthusiasm has been
of the highest class. The outstanding examples of
prompt aggressive action were the capture of the Fort
Pt. Minon and Fort De Mengaht.

C. H. GERHARDT,
MAJOR GENERAL, U. S. ARMY, Commanding.

September 29, 1944, France

Dearest Folks,
    I received my two bars so now I'm a
Captain. Already I've gained a good bit of
prestige and it means $36 more a month in the
bank.
    I went to church again last Sunday. I'm
quite a Christian now a days. This country
is one big apple orchard, every kind and

shape. I eat them all day long. I can't speak
French yet but I'm sure it's because I've
never tried. I think I'll learn to speak it.
I'm going to be here long enough.

I'll be able to write more often for a
while and you be sure and write me often. Oh
yes—get me about two dozen pairs of athletic
shorts, size 30, will you? That's underwear
you know. And get them and send them just as
soon as possible. I'm already out. By the
time you get this and I get a package it will
be a month and a half anyway so please don't
waste time in between. I'd sure like some
warm sheepskin gloves or mittens, too. A
really expensive pair, and a box of candy
bars, like "Oh Henry" or "Baby Ruth" or
"Snickers."

Boy I'm hungry and cold...not really, but
I sure would appreciate them. By Golly, I'd
like to eat pickles and pickled pigs feet and
green olives again. Well, I'll quit for now—
just want you to know I'm well and happy and
am thinking of you all the time. Don't forget
the underwear and be sure they are athletic
shorts. All my love, Charles.

September 30, 1944, France

Dearest Mother, Dad and Carmen,
Just another line to let you know I'm
doing OK and feeling great. I wrote you
yesterday and told you the same, but good
things can't come too often, I guess. While
I'm on the subject of yesterday, let me
remind you of that request for underwear
again...two dozen athletic shorts size 29 or
30 by the fastest return mail and a pair of
sheepskin lined gloves or mittens.

In a few minutes I'm going to have an
excellent dinner of turkey and cranberry
sauce, no kidding! Right now I'm with a
quartermaster outfit helping to guard some

```
of its food. Ha!!
    My company is spread out over 500 miles
and I'm going to have some job in a few days
to collect them. I've been to Cherbourg and
to Brest and many other large cities,
including Paris.
    I'm OK, doing all right and not too
unhappy. In fact except for being homesick,
I'm very happy. I'm a captain now and I also
have an A.P.O., so address my letters
different. All my love, Charles.
```

Following the Brest campaign, we moved by truck to Luxembourg. They had established depots for food and gasoline along the way. Sullivan gave the task of guarding them to A Company. So, it took better than half of my company to guard the depots all the way from Brest and along to Paris and then to Luxembourg. I put a couple of men at each depot. I came along behind as the Battalion cleared these places and picked up the men and the supplies that were left at each spot.

They had arranged for us to have our meals at various Air Force installations. But Quarter Masters pulled the trucks after several days. The Air Force reviewed its expenses and said they could allow only so much for transient meals. Transients would be anybody not part of that regular unit. Finally, they would no longer even allow us meals and just quit feeding us. So, we ended up taking a box car on a slow moving French train. We had no rations whatsoever. I had only picked up part of the company—two or three men at each depot. So, I ended up with something like 20 to 25 men at Versailles, just outside of Paris. I had the conductor on the train drop our car off and put it on a side track and leave it at Versailles. My runner and I hitchhiked our way into Paris. Paris was still off limits to any outside troops. We asked some people where headquarters was for the occupation army. Turns out that it was in a big hotel, with an enormous foyer, right on the famous Champs-

Elysee Avenue.

Well, we'd been on this blasted railway with these French engines burning cheap coal and billowing clouds of smoke over everything. We were black, our clothes were filthy, and we hadn't had a chance to wash. Hadn't had a shower in weeks. Just rough-looking as hell. My intention was to get transportation, probably a couple of 2 ½ ton trucks so that we could all go up to Luxembourg where the Battalion was. I was striding into this fancy hotel when, all of a sudden, I hear somebody roar out, "Ace!" followed by an expletive having something to do with my ancestors. It was Sullivan!

The Battalion had moved to Luxembourg, where they had quarters for them. Sullivan had just came down to Paris to get new orders. Here's Sullivan, with his long neck, standing about 6'5", all cleaned up with a fresh uniform and everything. So, I started to tell him about our terrible troop trials, how hard we had been trying. I explained that the Quarter Masters had taken the trucks away from us and that the Air Force had refused to feed us anymore.

Sullivan was just inflamed that people hadn't honored their commitment, so off we went to higher authorities. I remember Sullivan's red face and his Irish tongue going fast, his fist pounding the table top. Immediately we got trucks sent out to the box car to pick up the guys and bring them in.

The Red Cross was in Paris. They had hotel spaces, but only for Red Cross workers. My guys were put in a hotel but under the strictest observation. They could shower and a shave and get all shined up, but under no circumstances were they to hit the streets of Paris. Paris was a closed city for Allied troops at this time. The command units were there, but it was closed to field units.

We stayed at the hotel and got showered and shaved, even clean clothes. We were all slicked up again, but the guys couldn't stand not to be on the streets. So, the first thing they did was go down to loiter in front of the hotel. Well, the MPs were all over the place, particularly in Paris as there were Americans in there. One thing led to another. More MPs poured in and it led to a fight. They picked all the men up and hauled them to prison. Now we had a different problem. However, I got permission to pick them up in a truck and immediately take them out of Paris.

So, I was in Paris prior to it being an open city to everybody.

```
October 26
Belgium

Dearest Muriel, Ed and all,
    You can bet your life that I am going to
stay lucky. I give old Dame Luck all the help
I can of course and so far it works. However
there is no accounting for this strange
selection of who gets hurt and who doesn't.
    Write to me again and write often. All my
love, Charles
```

DRILL FOR CLEARING OF ISOLATED BUILDING

This drill is based on the organization of the Infantry squad consisting of the following:

1 Sergeant	Squad Leader
1 Corporal	2nd in command and grenadier
11 BAR Gunner	
1 BAR assistant gunner	
1 BAR ammo carrier and rifleman	
7 Rifleman	

I - the Approach:

The building should be approached as closely as possible using all available cover and concealment and at that time positions for the ASSAULT, SUPPORT, SUPPORT GROUP should be chosen and assigned by the squad leader.

II - SUPPORT GROUP:

This group consists of the corporal, 2nd in command, the BAR

V -

Consisting of two riflemen. These men move rapidly to the wall of the building under a covering fire from the support group and move under cover of the wall until they reach the point of entry, either a door or window. No. 1 entrymen uses the butt of his rifle to break down the door or window while No. 2 is prepared to throw in a grenade if necessary - If No 2 throws a grenade he steps inside immediately after the explosion and covers all exits from the hall or room. If it is not deemed necessary to throw a grenade he steps inside immediatley after the door or window has been broken down by No. 1.

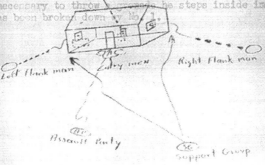

Chapter Twelve

Ludweiler and Lauterbach

In a squad of Rangers, everybody there whose responsibility it was to fire their weapon did it in the proper way with aimed shots.

—Ace Parker

FOR OUR NEXT mission, we became a part of General Patton's 3rd U.S. Army and were further attached to the 6th Cavalry Group for operations. We relieved a cavalry unit. A Cavalry unit consisted of light tanks, armored cars and that sort of thing. We took over their line and relieved an entire battalion with just one company. Our job was to keep track of what the Germans were doing and act as a blocking agent. This was shortly before the Battle of the Bulge.

It's amazing how little fire power they got out of a regular infantry platoon. In the infantry, with about a million men, one can't make a generalization that fits everybody. But abuses such as refusing to expose themselves long enough to take an aimed shot was widespread. If there were 15 or 20 men lined up in a group, they would maybe only get aimed shots from 5-10% of them. The rest would stick the gun over the thing and pull the trigger to make a noise. In a squad of Rangers, everybody there whose responsibility it was to fire their weapon did it in the proper way with aimed shots. That's why we could go in and relieve a much larger outfit and accomplish the same thing.

The unit we replaced had positioned automatic weapons where they didn't have an adequate sight to fire, except for what was right out in front of them. When we took over that area, we changed all that. We had to relocate the gun positions. Then we clipped a tree or shrub here and there, so we could see what was out in front of us before the Germans were on us. It was an area so large that we couldn't possibly man the whole thing. We formed a series of strong points and then patrolled vigorously out in front of us. Any advancement or probing of the Germans gave them the impression that we were heavily manned. So a small group of us could be more effective in the same defensive area than a much larger group of men.

It was night time and things were shut down. Our perimeter was set up so that we shot anything that moved. This was at a time when we had a lot of Germans coming in on us. I had to tell everybody, "You know where I am and you know that my bladder is pretty weak. I'm going to be going in and out of that hole, so make sure you're not shooting at me."

While we were up in that blocking position in a valley called the Ludweiler area, we got word that Headquarters needed some intelligence from a German artillery unit that was directing fire at us. We were ordered to try to get into the German headquarters and capture an officer along with any documents we could get our hands on.

The job was given to B Company to get the officer. Lt. Louis Gombosi, B Company Platoon Leader, picked a group from his platoon and arranged with the artillery to support the plan. The support artillery put a box of fire around the German headquarters. They knew right where it was. Gombosi and his group followed the artillery shelling in, grabbed the German senior officer and all the papers they could and destroyed the rest. They then followed the artillery fire out.

Gombossi was worried about rescue attempts from the Germans, since they would have been just furious about losing an officer, like bees when the nest is disturbed. And it was not even so much the officer as it was the plans he knew. The Germans would rather kill the officer than have him taken back and used as a gain for the Allies. Gombosi was coming back to our line and knew he was going to get a furious counterattack from the headquarters he'd just attacked. That's why the block of artillery surrounded them and protected them on the way out. It was a real tricky thing. The box of protection from the artillery was on three sides so nobody could get inside the box. The Germans would not be able to attempt a rescue.

Gombosi turned the German officer over to higher authorities at headquarters. We had a lot of tricky missions like that. At the same time, however, we were much used where we shouldn't have been.

On December 3, 1944, Company F was ordered to attack the town of Lauterbach, Germany. The objective was a row of houses about 300 yards away. The ground sloped gently down to the village and was relatively flat. They advanced across open ground, under a hail of mortar and small arms fire. The first assault wave left the woods on the run, across the open fields toward the town. They were exposed to enemy observation from the high ground to their front and on both flanks. Two hundred yards from the town's edge, this wave got hit by enemy machine guns, one gun firing from an emplacement on the left and two firing from an emplacement on the right.

From an exposed position on the forward slope of a hill, Private First Class Leo G. Samborowski, a BAR gunner, poured a full magazine burst into the two emplacements on the right, while his comrades found slight cover from the machine guns. He then ran forward until he could train his gun directly on the open emplacement, firing eight full clips of ammunition. He eliminated the machine gun. The machine gun on the right, however, focused solely on Samborowski and killed him by a hail of bullets, hitting him over 100 times. Leo G. Samborowski gave his life so that his comrades could reach the houses on the edge of town. He was awarded the

Distinguished Service Cross, and on August 20, 1998, he was admitted into the Ranger Hall of Fame for his heroism.

I remember a large open field. F Company had been ordered to cross this open field to get into its position and occupy the area. The Germans were strung out and ahead of them. In crossing the open field in broad daylight, they got caught by two machine gun nests which just tore F Company apart; plus a couple of tanks down there kept throwing artillery in along with some long-range machine guns.

A lot of guys were lying out there calling for help. I was ordered to take my company forward, go across the field and reinforce F Company. I looked out there. The Germans were just randomly firing and shelling the area. There had been enough activity with F Company coming out of the woods that the Germans suspected there were more American troops in there.

The shelling created an awful lot of tree burst. The shells would hit the tops of the trees and blow pieces of shrapnel and trees and everything else down around us. It was a very bad place to be. So when I got to this edge and saw these guys out there ahead of us on the ground, probably a dozen or more, I radioed back to Battalion Headquarters. I told Sullivan that I wasn't going to take my company across in daylight. The results wouldn't be any better than what they were for F Company, the men right out there in front of me. I said I believed that the Germans were not trying to advance. "I can't imagine that F Company is in any kind of trouble now," I said. "And if it gets that way, then we're here. But I will not take my men out across that field in daylight."

I got permission to wait until dark. The problem now was to stay on the edge of the woods so that we could observe things and make sure the Germans would not counterattack. And if they did, then we would know it. Occasionally we would throw some artillery fire down on them. I radioed back to the battalion the location on the maps. I wanted absolutely no sign whatsoever that there was any life on the edge of that field. And if there was, then we would just artillery them to death.

Under the pressure of lying there and hearing the voices of the stranded F Company men all day long—men who were wounded, thirsty, and frightened—a medic with me just broke down. Combat fatigue type of thing. That is, you lose control, become extremely fearful, and know you are going to die. So, I kept him right with me. We crossed only after the darkness blanketed us. When the action was over, the Allied tanks came up through the village from the rear and pulled us out. I then sent the medic back, and they sent him all the way home. He wrote later that he and his family had a mass said for me.

> Dear Captain Parker,
>
> Pardon me for addressing the envelope "Ace Parker." I don't know your first name so I used your cognomen. I received a letter from Mother and Dad last night and they had a mass said for you and Col. Sullivan and Lt. Askins and Souchier and Zilepski Christmas day and another for Company A. Both my parents and I remember you and the Rangers in our prayers. I feel it is a small way of repaying my thanks to you. I know that by holding in the woods that day, December 3, I think it was till way after dark and then moving across you saved my life along with others. I also remember well how you shared your coffee with me before we moved out and how you kept me with you that last day and night before we were pulled out for chow on December 6. It was a distinct honor to have served under you. I regret I can no longer do so. Wherever the army sends me I shall do my best. I'll never forget you or the Rangers.
>
> It doesn't make any difference if you are Catholic or not. If you wear the enclosed medal you'll be under God's protection. I'll

close now and sincerely hope we shall meet
back in the States where I can do something
concrete to show my thanks.
   Please take care of yourself and all the
others. With my best personal respects, Sir,
I remain—Jim Dorsey.

F Company Sgt. Christopher Jeffers came across the field
to our location on the edge of the woods and guided us back
across. We then went into the houses. I was so cold from lying
on the ground and not moving at all that I was just shaking.
We built a fire in the basement of one of the houses on the
cement floor. The house soon filled with smoke, however, as
there was no place for it to go. We laid on the floor to breathe
until we could organize and move out of there.

Tec 5, Jesse Tayler, our radio man, had brought the big
radio into the house and had set it up. Jesse, raw-boned, big
and strong, a Texan, was trying to reach Battalion
Headquarters. He extended the antennae up through a hole in
the ceiling, most likely made from bombing. He was just
sitting there when all of a sudden the radio started to rise up
from the floor. He pulled it down again, but to our amazement
the radio again began to rise. We looked at each other and
communicated with our eyes that someone was up there
pulling on that antennae—it couldn't be doing it all by itself.
So, we put a couple of bursts of fire through the ceiling and
others stormed up the stairs. Sure enough, a German soldier
was up there.

Wilbur Ingalls relates his memory of that night.

"Ace held us back from going across the field,
down into the houses until dark. Then we went in. He
got a guide to lead us. We held onto each other's back.
It was pitch dark to get into those houses. We stayed
in those houses all day.

"There was a Tiger tank that kept going up and

down the street. Finally, we got across the road and took more houses. We were down in the basement of one of the houses. In the meantime we had picked up a fellow who had volunteered, but apparently he wasn't a well trained soldier. He went crazy. He lost it. He would grab Ace and holler, 'There's 60 Germans out there!' His eyes were just bugged out.

"Ace was trying to keep him calm over in a corner. Late in the afternoon I remember us getting ready to go. The German machine guns were still operating. We had come from one way to enter the first houses and crossed the street into others. Then we were going out the back of those houses, down across and up into the woods. This is where the other company in our battalion was located that we had lost. We were getting ready to take off for the woods, but two machine guns were shooting up the valley. One was shooting tracers up high and the other one was shooting underneath it. It looked like you could run right under the high tracer bullet but the other one would come low chewing up dirt. Ace stopped everything. 'Guys, stay here just a second.' He got on the radio and reached somebody in another company to get fire on those machine guns and engage them until we could take off. But that's the way he would operate. He was always thinking. Of course, they engaged the machine guns and we made it across and up into the woods."

DEFENCE
CIRCLE

BN
CO

SKETCH MAP.
REF: Interview Capt Parker, ACO

ACO COUNTERATTACKED
1600 - 25 FEBUARY

KALFERTSHAUS

2ND

1ST

N

Chapter Thirteen

Battle of Irsch-Zerf

What was important in the Vietnam War was the body count; in World War II it was the land we took and held.

—Ace Parker

HALF THE MEN killed in the entire war were killed in nine days of fighting at the battle of Irsch-Zerf. It was a battle engaging the German SS 6th Mountain Division, a fresh unit only recently arrived from duty in Norway. It was the worst battle for us of the entire war, but it was truly a Ranger mission.

The action took place from February 23—March 4, 1945 and was cited as "one of the most successful Ranger operations of World War II." It was necessary to deny this area to the enemy to guarantee cover to the 10th Armored Division, and to assure that no enemy force would infiltrate after the Division had passed or be in position to launch counterattacks against the 94th Division bridgehead. To accomplish this the Corps Commander ordered us, the 5th Ranger Battalion, to move forward and occupy this area, to protect the passage of the 10th Armored Division around this corner, and deny the road net to enemy forces.

We had been patrolling when headquarters informed us, "We've got a message from Sullivan. We've got a hot one for you. Take everything that's your property. Get here and do it as quickly as you can. Do it now. Don't wait for your replacement. Just leave." We were to go to Taben Rodt and assemble, then on to Hoch's Hill where Sullivan waited for us with further orders.

We marched fast to get down to Taben Rodt. Even before reaching Taben Rodt, we had 24 men blasted out of my company (six men were killed and eighteen were wounded). That was more than a third of what I had!

Two wild rounds of German artillery landed in the front half of the company column and in that split second got both my officers. The blast hurled men in all directions. The injured were hurt by shrapnel and concussion. It knocked me down, flat on my face, with everything—shrapnel and debris from the blast, landing around me. But I was unhurt. I reported to headquarters that I had 24 inoperatives. We had to leave the wounded behind for the proper troops to pick up. Whoever was available and closest to pick them up would do so. We could only stay long enough to set it in motion. We couldn't stop—there was no time to indulge in regrets. We had a mission to do.

When someone died, I was truly distressed. But I didn't let that last. It's an expression of grief to shed a tear or two. It signified that this guy was valuable. He was our friend. The guys or I might take a few minutes and go over in our minds again what that person had meant to us; get it fixed in our memories the circumstances under which we had said good bye.

The company commander was in charge of sending the letters home when someone died. I wrote those letters myself. I tried to put the best and most accurate light on it that I could. Of course I included the things that they wanted to know— suffering, how and what killed them. If the man was wounded then he could write the letter himself when he was in the hospital.

Tech Sgts. James Rooney and Philipp Thomas, already trained in the job and carrying heavy responsibility, were made platoon leaders on the spot. By doing this, I lost these two men to field commissions. It happened to all the companies. In other words, we didn't want to bring other lieutenants in that we didn't know anything about. But now that they had been promoted, they might be transferred to another company where they would not be on such familiar terms with the men under them.

At Taben Rodt we loaded up with ammunition, food, and the mines that were allotted to every company. The mission's importance was determined by the fact that the road represented the route of many German reinforcements and must be denied at any and all costs. The men were advised to grab some hot chow and to travel as light as possible. Each man was issued extra gun ammunition, AT mines, and one K Ration and one D Ration. Confidence and determination were stamped on the face of each man.

Next we had to cross the Saar River and climb a hill. The engineers had managed to build a footbridge. Colonel Sullivan had already made the crossing on the foot bridge, had climbed the hill and was now at the top speaking with the division commanders to receive orders for our mission. Then he sent a runner with directions for us to follow.

The foot bridge held us as we ran, one by one, across the churning waters below. It was now 8:00 at night. Then we climbed that beastly hill. Of all the memories, everybody remembers that hill. It would break our hearts and blow our lungs getting up that darn thing, especially as loaded down as we were. We used our hands and knees and just leaned forward. We were drenched in sweat from the effort.

When we got up there, each sergeant automatically assembled his group and reported to the company commanders. Then I reported to Colonel Sullivan, "Company A is available and organized." We then received our orders for the mission from Sullivan. The mission was to disorganize the rear of the enemy defense to the Saar River bridgehead and to prevent reinforcements from using the Zerf road. This was a main road for the Germans. We were to infiltrate through German held territory. And between us and the target—

German troops. It was dark. It was loaded with hills and valleys covered with pine trees. The country was extremely rough. We had never seen it. We had never even seen a map of it. We were given an azimuth and were to advance by compass direction. Then we went back and briefed our people.

In the Rangers we told our men what was going on. They were briefed on missions. We were to hold this area for 48 hours until an infantry unit could reach us and relieve us. Unknown to us at the time, those 48 hours would turn into many days.

For nine consecutive hours we infiltrated through enemy lines, constant ascent and descent through intensely wooded hills; each man hanging on the very breath of his pal in front of him.

We walked about four miles to get to Zerf. We were always checking and rechecking the contour maps till we figured out where we were. We were traveling at night. It was dark. Pitch black. We were supposed to be in touch with the man ahead of us, but at the same time making no noise or sound.

At this point we weren't trying to make a lot of speed, we were just trying to make forward progress. In order to get from here to there we had to infiltrate our way through the German lines. We weren't big enough to get up in a line and march and kill everything in front of us. There were six companies. We were to move in two columns. A Company was heading up one column and D Company was heading up the other with George Miller.

We were in a box-like formation while moving. We didn't go in a straight line but at an angle through the German lines. That meant that we were exposed to more chances of getting caught. It was the best ground for traveling, however, to take us where we needed to go.

High velocity artillery fire, plus the difficult terrain, caused the two parallel columns to lose contact and broke the column of files in several places. We maintained contact by radio.

During our march, one platoon from B Company just flat got lost in the dark. They later connected with an armored tank infantry unit of the 10th Armored Division. They were used as tank infantry, scouting for the tanks and protecting them. Eventually they connected with us.

During the crossing of the creek bed, C Company sent a patrol to a road junction. They surprised the enemy and took 20 PWs (Prisoners of War). We still had 4000 yards to march through enemy territory before reaching our objective. The prisoners, despite all difficulties involved, had to be carried along with us. Before reaching our target, B Company would be guarding 85 PWs.

About dawn on the 24th of February, we had advanced to a place estimated to be half way to our destination. We were confused as to our exact location, so Sullivan called a halt. Patrols were sent out to locate the position, but this proved unsuccessful. We called for the artillery to place two rounds on our objective. The passing shells oriented us and we started north for our goal.

We encountered a cluster of houses along the way—seven of them. It was a typical little European hamlet. Sullivan said, "I wonder what's in them." So he sent a patrol of five men to investigate. A runner was sent back relating there were no German soldiers occupying the buildings, only a few civilians. Sullivan said that this may be a good place to hole up—get some sleep. We could get a hot meal in us and then move on. B company put the German prisoners (soldiers) in the basement. We separated and moved into the buildings.

"Pete" Gunnoe S/Sgt. of B Company, wrote some memories to Lt. Stan Askin years later. He related this story in the letter:

> There were several adults, women and
> children and one old man. One of the children
> was his eight year old grandson. I kept
> telling this little boy that we were not

going to hurt him or his grandpa if they
would just keep quiet and not go outside. As
fate would have it, that little boy turned up
in the USA in 1969 and of all places in
Huntsville, Alabama as an engineer with
McDonald Douglas Corporation in the Space
Program where I was working for NASA as a
quality engineer. I was working at their
plant one day in 1969, checking over some
specifications for the Saturn Program that
they were developing when this young man
said, "You were with the Rangers near Trier,
Germany. You, who come to our home one
morning and put us in the basement. I'm that
little boy you talked to." As I took a long
look at his face I could see the face of that
child in this young man 24 years later.

We moved on. We got to a road at the bottom of the next
valley. While my Company was crossing a stream bed, a patrol
of approximately 10 Germans came down the road. My
Company fired on them and they quickly withdrew. Soon after,
a German Red Cross vehicle, a white jeep, came sailing down
the narrow dirt road. We hailed them. It was a German doctor
and 4 medical aid men. The doctor was in complete
amazement since he still thought he was four kilometers
behind his front lines.

He flatly refused to believe that these men were Americans.
He rationalized they were German troops in American
uniforms preparing to infiltrate the American lines as so many
of the enemy had done during the Battle of the Bulge.
According to him, it was absolutely impossible that an
American force could have reached a point so far behind the
German lines without fighting. He finally did become
convinced and they surrendered. He had no choice. He helped
us with our medical care thereafter. He was a doctor long
before he was a member of the army. We had no doctor with
us for the mission since ours had refused to go with us. Capt.

Thomas Petrich was his name. By this time Petrich had decided that he had been through a lot of this darn stuff, landing and the whole thing. He had put his time in and thought, "I'm nothing but a glorified aid man." He wanted to get back to the medical unit. He felt he was losing his skills. So we went in with no doctor. Then they flew in the medical officer, Capt. Joe Hilsman. He came in at Kalfertshaus. A lot of things happened at Kalfertshaus. He came into a real mess.

Kalfertshaus was the farm house that we came across just a little south of our target, the Irsch-Zerf crossroad. This building gave us a chance to rest and regroup. While holding up here, Capt. Byrne, the intelligence officer of the battalion, was examining a German bazooka-type weapon that he had just found. It was a long tube that shoots a grenade much like a rocket. A fella had to make sure nobody was behind him when firing the thing because the flame would shoot out of the rear of it like crazy. The explosive in this weapon is capable of blowing a track off a tank or the side of a building. Capt. Byrne was looking down through the muzzle end. Maybe he plunked it down, I'm not sure, but it went off and blew his head off.

We finally reached our target. We looked over the terrain to decide where we were going to place the battalion so as to deny that road to the Germans. Once that was determined, we distributed ourselves around and dug in. My company was to be at the lower or southern end of the circle. We would be facing the woods that we had just walked out of. Sullivan dispersed the rest of the companies around the perimeter.

E Company dug mines down into the roadway and camouflaged them. Then they got rid of any disrupted dirt. The pin had a ring on it. The ring was pulled. Now it was armed. They were set so that when a tank or car drove over them they would blow. A man could walk across them without detonating them, however. We expected that in 48 hours the division would be up there to relieve us. Well, they didn't.

Some of the Germans knew we were there and targeted us. But a lot of the Germans coming in were totally surprised, since they were retreating from the same places we had just come from.

Prior to my company's placement at the edge of the woods, we were ordered to hold two pillboxes, one south of the crossroads and the other further south of Kalfertshaus. During the middle of the afternoon we were suddenly counter-attacked from the woods by a force of approximately 200 men heavily armed with automatic weapons and Panzerfaust. We were pinned down. The enemy advanced within range of a hand to hand fight with grenades and close in automatic weapon fire. We held our ground for about 45 minutes after which the Germans broke and withdrew. We pulled back to the Kalfertshaus where we prepared to take up position for the night. However, we were counterattacked again by the same enemy unit which attempted to cut us off from the rest of the Battalion. The enemy's leading man was killed and the rest dispersed. During this attack, we had three casualties and estimated that we had killed 50 to 60 enemy. Col. Sullivan decided that our position was too exposed and called us back to take up positions at the south flank of the defense circle.

At one time E company, on the southwest corner of the circle, ran out of ammunition, and was attacked by an overwhelming force of approximately 400 men. They were being pushed back. They only had five men left. My company was told by Sullivan to take 12 men up and try to hold the line where E Company had been overrun. So we got up there and now had fox holes with my 13 men and their five. The Germans could smell victory in taking some ground back. That's when we called the artillery fire in on us from the 284th.

The 284th Artillery was back across the river we had just crossed. They were up on higher ground than we were, Hocher's Hill, so they could see the entire area.

We had a connection with the 284th artillery. The mission

was important enough that the 284th was assigned to support only us at that time. We could call on them for artillery drops whenever we needed to. They gave us an artillery observer, positioned with us, that could direct them. An artillery observer is talking the same language that the artillery people are. That way we could utilize the artillery to the best of our advantage. They had the same maps as their observer. So the observer could say, "Direct fire on these coordinates" where we wanted the shell to land.

During the day we oriented the map for the north and used coordinates of longitude and latitude. He would say, "Lift the thing!" and then they would quit. Or if the last shell fell exactly where we wanted it to, then he would say, "Fire for effect!" Then every gun in the place lit up on that location and fired. They may fire three shells from each gun, but a blanket of fire power descends on that target. It breaks up all the resistance if you are lucky and if the enemy is not dug in too well. If you get up to the location fast enough after the barrage, you've got them. You don't want to give them any time to shake all that off.

Anyway, the artillery questioned our request for fire on that particular position. "What's going on out there?" they asked. Now remember, they had been firing at the Germans when the Germans had occupied these holes. Capt. McPartland, the artillery liaison observer with us, made the request clear for artillery to fire on his position. The observer yelled to us when he got the report that the shells were on their way. We slipped into our narrow-slit trenches and let the above ground Germans absorb the shelling. We got as far forward as possible in those foxholes. I was sitting down there, squeezing on in. The artillery dropped down on us in one huge effort. Dirt was flying! Now we're in the holes and the Germans were on their feet; they had to be because they were the ones attacking. They attacked right on through us, however, so we just turned to our rear and started shooting them. We killed an enormous number of Germans that way. That artillery fire sure did help!

The attack progressed to a close in fight with the enemy force. After a confused fight in pitch darkness and close cedar undergrowth, E Company drew back. Some of the men were surrounded and taken prisoner. It was impossible to identify between friendly and enemy troops. The only way to identify small arms fire was to recognize the difference between the sound of friendly or enemy weapons.

F Company was sent up to regain the lost ground. My company moved back to its place at the south flank of the circle.

During the day we dropped artillery concentrations on the enemy and killed an estimated 100 Germans.

The following morning, February 28, at 0600 (6 AM), an enemy company attempted to penetrate our defense circle from the southwest, moving quietly into the undergrowth. We were warned of this infiltration by the growling of a St. Bernard dog who was by now our "mascot."

We were more in the open than the other companies, occupying a large pasture. We were facing the woods all the way around. There was a dog running around. The dog was a big breed. I've always thought of him as a St. Bernard, and a young dog. We fed him, of course. We didn't have much to feed him. We would take some food away from the German prisoners. Anyway, he'd get a little food once in a while. And of course the whole blasted place was going up in fire and explosions, which made the dog cringe.

That dog aided us without knowing it. In the early morning the Germans were making counter-attacks on us. We didn't hear anything, but he did. So, he would growl low down in his throat and he would look out where he thought the disturbance was coming from. His smell and hearing were much better than ours. The pup was able to alert us on several occasions. It would be hard to estimate how many of our lives the dog saved.

Sadly, the dog was eventually killed. Lou Gombosi hated to see the dog die. He wrote in a letter, again to Stan Askin, many years later:

> The Germans hit us in a barrage of rockets (Screaming Memies). You could see them coming. Trees, soil, rocks and smoke were all over the terrain, a few hundred feet from us and between the separated Rangers. It looked like the final days on earth. In front of us was a beautiful St. Bernard pup, running back and forth, apparently left behind by the enemy. As we made our way through the barrage, I saw the dog laying dead near one of the rocket craters. Being a farmer, I loved animals. Seeing dead enemy never phased me. It was a shame and sad to see this beautiful dog dead. The rocket and artillery attacks never ceased all night. All the trees were a littered shamble around our position. We repulsed all counterattacks with heavy enemy casualties.

Another letter to Stan Askin, this one from S/Sgt. Pete Gunnoe, reveals this memory:

> The morning at the junction of the Irsch-Zerf road, when those German tanks started rolling, I can still hear those engines roaring up the hill toward where we were waiting down in a ravine in ambush near the junction. I had a machine gun set up to cover the men with the bazooka. I can still see those Jerries popping out of those tanks. Boy, when they were hit by the bazooka they wasted no time getting down the road. They didn't know what happened. I also remember another evening. We could see a large patch of pine woods on a hill across

the ravine which was being filled with what
looked like a whole German Army. We waited
until they got in and settled down. Then the
artillery (from the 284th) started coming in
and the noise was like hell. Those Jerries
sure got wiped out that night because the
next morning the pine woods were gone and the
German soldiers' bodies were stacked up like
railroad ties. Another evening—late, we were
attacked by Germans and our machine guns ran
out of ammo and Germans were everywhere all
over us. One German jumped in the hole on top
of me. Fortunately, I shot him before he shot
me. I still have that gun.

One morning before daylight, we were
attacked from our left flank again. We held
fire until they were right on us before the
CO gave orders to fire. By that time those
Jerries looked like giants! One of my best
buddies was up front of the machine gun
position. I gave orders for them to pull back
before I opened fire with the machine gun. I
guess he didn't hear me. The Jerries just
kept coming like we weren't even firing. My
buddy finally did try to get up and was cut
down by my machine gun. I later became a
Section Eight case for quite a long, long
time over this.

Another time we were being attacked, I was
ordered to move a machine gun up to the
front. We no more than got there and got the
gun on the ground when we found ourselves
surrounded by Germans. My two men were hit
and as I tried to get to the gun I was hit
for the 5th and last time. My helmet and
sweater were riddled with holes but I made it
to the aid station. Although, on my way there
I almost got shot by one of our men. Lucky
for me I heard a bolt click and saw his face
in the moonlight before I hollered out to him
that it was me.

Inside the bunker, the German Doc that we

> had taken prisoner on our way into this Hell
> hole told me I had been hit with a pistol
> grenade. He said, in broken English, "I got
> no needle, no shot for pain, but I have a
> bottle of German wine." He opened it and
> said, "Drink all down and don't stop until
> all gone!" I did as he said and went out
> like a light. When I came to I was in a frame
> house, hurting and sick as hell as I'd only
> eaten what nuts and weeds I'd found besides
> the one D ration bar that I had in my shirt
> pocket which was all I needed for a 48 hour
> mission, not a 10 day siege. I vaguely
> remember someone saying that half tracks
> were coming for the wounded.

It was raw—cold. No special clothing was issued back then for the cold. They do now. We were all young, vital, generating our own heat. It wasn't even an option to light a fire at Zerf. They would've blanketed the area with gun fire.

The mission was successful by our sheer determination, but it also would not have been possible without the support of the artillery unit assigned to us. This was a vicious and tenacious fight that we would not have survived without the enormous fire power of the 284th Field Artillery Division. Every artillery piece they had was for our use and our use only.

The Army Historical Division interviewed the 284th Artillery Division with the code name "Helpmate" following the battle. Part of that dissertation reads as follows:

> The next eleven days were destined to constitute the most glorious and heroic period of Helpmate's combat history. Teamed with the rough, tough, capable 5th Ranger Battalion, the 284th was to play a major role in the breakout from the Saar River bridgehead at Saarburg and Serrig.
>
> The 284th was selected as the field artillery battalion to provide direct artillery support for the

Ranger operation. The battalion was directed to send forward one liaison party and three forward observer teams to accompany the Ranger battalion....The liaison and forward observer teams left the battalion area to report to the Rangers at Taben, a village close to the Saar River crossing point.

Dawn came on the 4th, with the Rangers dug in on their objective. Helpmate was now firing at maximum range. Helpmate's work began as soon as the enemy discovered that the Rangers were dug in, in rear of their defensive positions. Fire missions began coming in from the forward observers and the Freudenburg area reverberated as the howitzer's sent their shells screaming over the lines. It was obvious from the start that Helpmate, by itself, could not furnish all of the artillery support needed by the Rangers. The fire direction center of the 284th was soon calling upon the other battalions of corps artillery to assist and their response was a welcome addition to the fire power of the battalion.

For artillery people, the only enemy fire they run into is counter battery. If the Germans had been able to triangulate and locate exactly where the artillery unit was located, they would have fired back at them. That's called counter battery. Then the two artillery units would be fighting each other. That could get real messy. Normally artillery people don't get into the bloody end of this thing. They are back ten to twelve miles and are hurling their shells as you ask for them, if you have a radio network that ties you in with them. On counter battery fire, there may be some shrapnel that flies around and lands in close enough to wound some artillery people. Normally they don't get killed. But they had one man killed and several wounded at Zerf.

These attacks continued for several days.

It becomes a little bit of a kaleidoscope, for specifics of time and exact place and things like that. You come away with an impression; you remember certain parts of this thing and then you tie them together. It may not have been exactly as it happened. The gist of it is right. The sequence and time and such, you can get whether it's morning or afternoon or night or day. And most of the time what day it was. But some of that you don't get straight in your mind. After all, it was over 54 years ago.

Burton Ranney of Company F remembers the mission as "one of the biggest things that I have done or been a part of." He wrote this in a letter to Stan Askin:

> I remember very well watching as cub planes dropped supplies to us. Rifle fire kept them high enough that it made it hard to hit our small area. A lot of the material was damaged. One of the craziest things that I remember and have told many times was when A and F Companies were told to take some high ground to our north. We called for so many rounds of artillery on that position and then we counted them and as the last one was coming in, we attacked up the hill. When we reached the top the Germans were still in their holes, and as they realized what had happened, they raised their weapons to fire and were shot immediately. In a few minutes there were two shots fired from a brush pile concealing a small vehicle of some kind that had a small cannon on it. Then the vehicle started his engine and made a 180 degree turn and sped away. I think he was as scared as we were. As a result of this firing from the vehicle every one started running for the trees to our left. I mean everyone! The Germans and us were running side by side because we didn't want anything to do with artillery of any kind. As a final they all became our prisoners. I laugh every time I

```
think of that episode.
     It was a horrible experience—to have a
perimeter and then to be attacked many times
not knowing when or where the Germans were
going to attack. It affected me somehow, to
the extent that afterwards, I could not sit
down and write a letter home for over a
month. My parents were so concerned that they
made inquiries as to what had happened to me.
```

Lines of communication had broken down pretty badly within the German army. We'd fight a patrol or a group of Germans going someplace. The battle would be with this group and that's where it ended. But they failed to get the information to other German units. So the German officers could not put together enough intelligence to say, "Jeez! We've got Americans coming and fighting in here!"

The Germans were now retreating. They had lost some ground. They were moving back deeper into Germany from France. And now they didn't know that we were here until they hit us. We held our fire until they were right on us and then every automatic fire that we had opened up on them. It was foggy and dark and we just mowed them down. We were a dagger that struck into them and then occupied that area. They had to go through the area in order to get out. And they also had to go through that area in order to reinforce up at the front line.

It devastated them so, that many of them just surrendered. Their morale was down. There were Germans giving up and there were Germans that were fighting desperately. It was a whole screwed up, mixed up mess. And lots of it in the dark and fog which was what made it such a marathon. "Pete" Gunnoe S/Sgt. recollected that the Germans were "coming up to us begging to be taken prisoner. We kept trying to get rid of them but they just kept following us saying, 'Me prisoner.' We finally had to knock them down to get away from them."

A group of 145 Germans approached our perimeter. We seized the opportunity to catch an unalert enemy in a hasty ambush and allowed the Germans to walk right up to us before opening fire. Seeing no escape, they threw down their weapons and surrendered.

We also had to be careful of the ammunition because we were running low and we didn't have any new coming in. We were low enough that it was starting to really bother us. We would tell each man to be careful and not be careless on firing.

We pulled the ammo from the BAR. A Browning Automatic Rifle goes off as long as you hold the trigger back. It has a cyclic rate of something like 450 cycles per minute. You can't really operate it that way but theoretically that's what it's capable of. If we did that we'd probably burn out the carbine. The Browning was an automatic and the M-1 was a semiautomatic. The M-1 was more conservative of shells. We could fire the M-1 one shot at a time. The shells for the BAR are the same size as the rifle shell. The BAR had a bipod up front to steady it. We would have been on our bellies behind it firing. It could be very steady. If we were firing our rifle, our rifle might waver a little bit and throw off the shot. But if we were firing the BAR from the hip then we weren't as steady.

The corporals and the sergeants were constantly checking on ammunition. They would ask, "How are you doing on ammunition?" The reply might be, "I've got three clips." (There are eight shells in a clip.) We had to constantly know what our ammunition situation was, because now we're in the fight. We can't phone back and say, "Ship some stuff up to us." We were in the battle and the Americans that supplied the troops were not with us because we were behind the German lines. And fire power was the only thing that was going to keep the Germans off our backs.

All of these things take place over a period of time. There are periods that nothing is going on. Not a thing. Maybe several hours in a row. Then all of a sudden all hell would break loose. A group of Germans, not knowing that we were there, would come through. And we pulled a surprise on them. Sometimes they knew we were there and were trying to break their way through. We were just sitting there and were not going to move. It was a very, very hard battle to fight.

I remember Bernard Peper, from Minneapolis, a Captain from Company B, was tossed around by so much noise from Nebelworfers, that he had to be relieved. Nebelworfers were huge, thin-skinned German rockets that didn't penetrate hardly anything. However, when they landed it was an enormous explosion. It would toss everything around. Bernie got caught in a barrage of it up there at Irsch-Zerf and didn't know where he was.

Another incident that happened shook us all up, Joe Drodwill in particular. I always told Joe, one of my sergeants, that he was one of the best field sergeants I ever had. Joe came up to the CO area and wanted to get warm. He had been taking watch in one of the fox holes. I asked him, "Who's got your hole?"

"Ted's taking over for me."

"OK, fine."

Ted was a straight arrow. I mean this kid was slim, good-looking and tall. He was married, going to attend college, and the whole bit. Well, an artillery shell came in—in a barrage, right into that foxhole and blew. It killed Ted. Tore him apart. He was a real loss. The minute that Joe found that out, he just flipped his lid. Joe roared off toward the enemy line. A couple of men ran out, before I even knew about it, tackled him, took his rifle away and dragged him back. They told me about what had happened. In the mean time, a couple of the guys took care of that fox hole and Ted.

Our medic, John Burke, told us later that he remembers talking with Ted Walters that same night. "Ted was wounded on D-Day and had just returned to us. We were joking that he should not get paid because he spent all his time in the hospital, not on the line. Someone then said the guy on outpost for Company A should be relieved. And Ted volunteered. Within the hour Ted was killed."

So, from then on in I kept Joe with me, until we could get him back and get him medical treatment. I can't remember how many days passed before we were able to get him into the hands of the medics. For the time being, he had lost it. I would talk to him about it. I told him that he had no real right to expect that he was God. He was not in charge of who did leave this earth and who didn't and under what circumstances. He did what he did. And it happened that it cost Ted. If it hadn't, then it would've cost him. The shell was going to come there. It wasn't that anybody showed themselves or attracted attention to it. I told him that I was going to need his stripes and somebody else would have to be in charge. That would make him a private before he left us. Joe eventually went back over to England and talked to the psychiatric people. Then they finally sent him back to us. He didn't have to go to the ZI, the Zone of the Interior, which was the name for the United States. If you went all the way back to the United States, then you stayed there. Hardly anybody came back after going there.

The 10th Armor Division finally arrived. We had accomplished our mission, though at great cost. We had suffered 90 casualties but had killed an estimated 299 enemy and taken 328 prisoners. It was said that we contributed to the collapse of the enemy's front.

The Americans now controlled all the ground behind them. They were now able to go right on into Zerf and then continue east on a broad front. The first ones to go through were the 10th Armor. The Germans didn't have a fixed line at that point. They were disorganized; their command structure was gone. Their supply was also all screwed up. We kicked them out and took prisoners.

The historians have told about the first 4 or 5 days of the Irsch-Zerf battle. But they missed a big part of the mission. There were two pill boxes that we had bypassed on the way in. Sullivan told us we had to go back where we came from and take those pill boxes. I remember I sat there and thought, "Should I just tell him to hell with this army career? How can I ask my men to turn around and do this all over again?" George, Company D Commander, who had also been given the assignment, told me later that he was thinking the same thing. We told Sullivan that we wanted to figure out a plan.

The 94th Infantry Division had laid out a series of objectives, but due to severe opposition and the low effective strength of its forces, they had been unable to take one of them—Hill No. 3. It was positioned 2000 yards south of the positions we had been holding.

We, A and D Companies, attacked abreast leading up to the hill. The heavy cedar undergrowth allowed the attack. In two hours we were within 200 yards of our hill objective. At this point, two tanks that were traveling with us were halted by mines and AT fire. D Company was pinned down by machine gun fire from a bunker on the forward slope of the hill. My company continued our advance swinging around to the right, outflanked the bunker and took 50 prisoners. F Company came up on the right of us and the lines were tied in across the trail. We were subjected to rocket barrage of 50 to 60 rounds, and sporadic SP and some mortar fire. Col. Sullivan called for us to pull back. (One PW later captured said that the 24th Mountain Division, which was the unit fighting the Rangers, had by this time a personal grudge and were simply out to destroy the Ranger Battalion.) During the night, Miller and I worked out a plan with Lt. Smallings, the forward observer from the 284th Artillery Division. The plan called for intermittent fire in heavy concentrations on the hill objective during the night.

The artillery people carried big radios. The artillery observer would direct the shelling exactly by use of good maps. We were pretty good with the artillery ourselves. We called for the Americans to drop artillery and sweep the valley intermittently and randomly up the hill in the most logical approach areas, to deny any movement there. When we got up into our old positions we had them throw a big barrage in. Up to the pill boxes all night long they fired. It might be ten minutes between a couple of shells in there and then it might be 15 minutes later and a whole slew of shells were dropped in. The shells landed as if just walking up through the woods and then landed right on top of the pill boxes.

While it was still dark, we, A and F Companies, positioned ourselves approximately 300 yards from our objective.

At 0600 an artillery barrage was laid. Then Captain Miller rolled an artillery barrage in. The field artillery hit the pillbox with a final concentration of fire. When they lifted the fire we were already within 3 or 4 minutes of the pillboxes. The two companies followed the barrage at less than 100 yards. We, A Company, hit the pill box with assault fire. Eight Germans found outside were cut down by automatic fire and the pillbox door was broken down. I think I pulled out about 50 men. The enemy were all inside in various stages of undress, shoes unlaced, clothes awry. It was early in the morning and they were getting themselves ready. The Germans didn't expect us since they thought this was just another round of artillery landing on them as it had been for the last five, six, seven hours. They didn't even have the doors locked. Nobody reached for their guns. If they had, they would've been shot. Forty-seven men and four officers were taken prisoner. My company had entered the pillbox five minutes after the final barrage had been lifted and had suffered no casualties.

F Company moved down quickly through enemy positions using assault fire and dropping grenades into enemy foxholes. They used their Tommy guns on any German activity they could see. Between 40-50 Germans were killed by F Company and they took 50 PWs.

After the first pillbox had been cleared, 12 men of A Company continued to the crest of the hill to what we thought was a second pillbox. This, however, turned out to be a water reservoir, with dug in positions around it. Fifteen more PWs were taken.

Just after the hill was taken, the enemy laid in artillery concentrations. I herded the PWs out of the pillbox where they were being held and placed them in the open along the road. I ordered the ranking officer to call his headquarters (there was still telephone communication from the pillbox). I said, "Tell them that the Americans will be shielded from their fire, but you and your men will not be." The German officer was so anxious to get out of there that he insisted that we march them to the rear. He wanted to get out of there because he didn't know how long his own artillery would hold fire. He didn't want his own artillery landing on them. It would've torn them apart out there in a bunch like that. So we told him, "Call your artillery people if you have a connection. Tell them what the situation is. Tell them that it will be landing on you and not us."

The enemy ceased fire and we dug in. When our positions were set we released the prisoners. Apparently the enemy had been observing our activity. Just as the PWs were moved down the slope, the enemy artillery came in.

That afternoon B and C Companies came to relieve us, A and F Companies. My company went to the rear bunker and prepared to get a good night's rest. We had been there about 20 minutes and were just falling asleep when word came that B and C companies had received a counterattack. We arrived at the hill at 10:00 PM. We remained in reserve positions. During the day, 3 March, an enemy patrol circled around and attempted to infiltrate our line. Three of the enemy patrol actually got into our foxholes but were shot using automatic fire.

The next night we were relieved. My company came out of this operation with one officer and 24 men. We had started the mission with approximately 52 men. Of the original 72 men that landed on D-Day, only 12 of those were still standing able to fight.

George Miller showed me a piece of paper I kept, a recommendation for me to receive a Bronze Star Medal. It read:

>Charles H. Parker, while serving with the Army of the United States, distinguished himself by heroic achievement in the Saarburg bridgehead area. The 28th February 1945, the 5th Ranger Battalion succeeded in infiltrating four kilometers behind enemy lines. Their location was detected and the unit was subjected to concentrated Artillery, Nebelwerfer, plus small arms fire. While advancing, the unit engaged a highly armed combat patrol. Capt. Parker immediately swung his company into an attack, personally directing his men against the attacking force, unhesitatingly going from man to man urging them on and bolstering up any imminent weak point. He then advanced forward, with complete disregard for his own personal safety, and succeeded in silencing a machine gun which had been responsible for many casualties, and the delay in the forward movement of the unit. His actions are slated with the highest of the armed forces.

1st German army after surrender by Germany in Summer of 1945. Near at in Markdt-Graffing.

Chapter Fourteen

Armistice Is Signed

They announced that the armistice had been signed.
May 5, 1945. We turned our truck lights on for the
first time in a long, long, long time.

—Ace Parker

AFTER ZERF WE were trucked to Luxembourg for a rest. The Germans weren't shooting at us here. We never traveled by trains. The French however continued to use the trains in areas where they could. The Allies so dominated the air, that they had no fear of Germans bombing the trains.

There was some patrolling we needed to do, because there were Germans, die-hards, that were around in the woods. This was near the end of the war. The only enemy movement was little knots of Germans roaming here and there refusing to give up. When that was reported we would send some men out. So, there was a little action there. But as an organized resistance the war was done.

About that time we got word that Roosevelt had died. That was April 12, 1945. I remember that I stood there and cried when I heard the news.

Then, against my will, Sullivan gave me a mission to take a truckload of soldiers to a rest camp in Theonville, France. But I had a pretty good deal going with one of the nurses from a nearby American field hospital. I was squiring her around and we were going to dances and such. You're damn right, I wanted to be where the fun was! And the fun was in Luxembourg. I sure didn't want to take someone back to a blasted recreation camp with organized games and Red Cross cookies. But I did.

This camp was run by a major, a large place with games, dances and the whole bit. The local girls would come in to dance. My guys, however, got drunk and broke a glass door. This wasn't just a standard-size window glass but was as long as this prissy administrative-type major could make it. He had scoured France to get this particular glass.

It also happened that we had to take a pistol away from one of the French girls, the kind of pistol that is small enough to fit in your hand. One of the guys was squiring a blonde girl to the dance. A beautiful little Algerian girl came in. When he saw this beautiful Algerian French girl with her dusky skin, big eyes and dark hair, he switched his allegiance real fast. The blonde pulled out this pistol and started shooting, taking a couple of shots at this fella who was escorting her. That was the straw that broke the camel's back! The major told me to get my damned outlaws out of there. "You think you combat guys are so damn smart. You got all this freedom when you are up there at the front. You don't have to follow regulations. You get all the best souvenirs. I don't get any souvenirs." We had several more days that we could have stayed there, but now we were on our way home.

On the way back from the rest camp, we heard on the radio that the war was over. They announced that the armistice had been signed. May 5, 1945. We turned our truck lights on for the first time in a long, long, long time. Then we noticed the lights were coming on all over. Wherever they heard the news, people would pull the shades up out of the way to let the light inside and to let the light shine out. The cars put their lights on. The lights of trucks came on. The lights went on all over Germany.

One of my lieutenants and good friend following the war, Stan Askin, became a writer for NBC radio. He wrote hundreds of scripts for them. During our army years together he was always taking notes. I guess it was his destiny to become a writer. Just recently the following manuscript describing his memory of the victory announcement was sent to me by his son. I must say, it is quite a memory. It deserves to be a chapter all by itself.

5th Ranger Officers (not all present) taken September, 1945, just prior to shipping home
Top photo: Lt. Stan Askin.

Chapter Fifteen

Pour Le Victoire,
A Memoir Of V-E Day

by Stan Askin

WE HEARD THE news on a quiet afternoon in May and somebody said, "Jesus Christ, men, we've got to celebrate tonight." And he took not the name of the Christian Lord in vain, for holy of holies, the Goddamned war was over.

Heal the wounds and mark the graves; hire double shifts at the prosthetics factories. What the young men had wrought in blood and bone the old men could now commence to put awry. For wasn't that the time-honored privilege of old men?

But now the last shot had been fired in anger — or fear — on this continent at least, and that was reason enough for rejoicing. Hitler's Festung Europa was kaput, having fallen considerably short of its proclaimed millenium. I took a long, deep breath and slowly as that small fist of vague tension somewhere deep in the viscera loosened its grip.

We were in a Replacement Depot outside of Le Havre on our way back to our units at the front from hospitals in England, and suddenly we began to feel like tourists. We would fight no more in this man's war; the grey festering hand of death hovered over us no longer. And tonight the jungles of the Pacific would be far away.

The word had not come in any of the ways I imagined it might during the days, nights, months, and seasons that grind out a year of combat and convalescence. I had lain in slit trenches, ditches, shattered farmhouses, and captured pillboxes-dry, hard, mud-filled, and snow-covered — from Omaha Beach to the Siegfried Line and the laboring heart of the Fatherland, during moments of relative safety, and wondered about my chances of survival...

First there had been the horror of D-Day on the beaches and cliffs of Normandy: "Come spend your June holiday at lovely, picturesque Vierville-sur-Mer, Vierville-by-the-Sea, an experience you will never forget."

And now a frightful year later, I stood with a group of strangers who shared only the same uniform and listened to the rotund voice of the British Prime Minister announce to the world in deep rolling tones that the Third Reich had succumbed to blood, sweat, and tears.

The loudspeaker was strung between two trees outside the Replacement Depot's Post Exchange shack. Some men sat on their haunches, eyes boring into the barren ground, while others stared directly at the loudspeaker, as if it were an instrument of the Almighty. There was no cheering, no crying. Those reactions we left for the folks back home. Here everyone was intent and quiet, slowly adjusting to the realization that we had made it, that we had lived to see the day, that we had lived so long. The exhilaration would come soon, when the numbness wore off.

By supper time there was a touch of euphoria in the air and we breathed deeply. It was New Year's Eve and the night lay before us. But New Year's Eve without date or destination for beyond the ugly camp was the ugly seaport of Le Havre and even that, which beckoned now like Paris, was barred to us on this night of our deliveries.

By the time we reached the mess tent our spirits were dampened by the fact of our confinement and the nature of the repast lying soggily before us in our metallic mess kits. Between the Spam and the canned fruit salad the lieutenant sitting across from me, an All-American type late of Stanford, pushed away his mess kit with a gesture reeking of disgust.

"Is this a meal fit to be set before conquerors on the night of their victory?"

"Hell, no!" said his friend in the next seat. "Not when we just made the world safe for democracy again."

"I wonder what the losers are eating tonight?" I said.

"Probably the same as us, if I know my armies," replied the Stanford man.

I had met Johnny DeWitt when our replacement company was organized in England. Johnny's friend was Doug Lawrence, a rather tentative lieutenant who would never rank with George Catlett Marshall as one of the more illustrious products of the Virginia Military Institute.

Johnny and Doug palled around together not because they had so much in common but because there was no one else in our group with whom either had as much to talk about. Their similar social background provided a frame of reference and an agenda for discussion and disputation: Southern versus Pacific Coast football; the comparative susceptibility of sorority girls, non-affiliated coeds, and town girls of the lower classes; the practice of racial and religious exclusion in fraternities (Johnny always took the more liberal view); the relative contributions of professional and civilian soldiers in wartime; English girls, French girls, German girls, miscellaneous girls. And this particular evening they speculated on the girls of Le Havre.

From time to time the conversation was punctuated by the sound of raucous gunfire from the direction of the harbor. After one especially joyous salvo, Doug said, "Man, that's the happiest soundin' shootin' I ever did hear! It must be Bastille Day and the Fourth of July rolled into one great big ball out there. Can't you just see those pretty little girls runnin' around up and down the streets lookin' for us handsome liberators?"

"Shut up and eat your goddamn fruit salad," came a voice from across the tent. "That's the only can you'll get into tonight."

Our nemesis was an old World War I retired general who had been pushed out of his combat command after taking a bad licking from younger generals in the Tennessee Maneuvers. Eventually assigned to command the rear areas of the European Theater of Operations, he undertook to facilitate administration and discipline by making life miserable for all those who came within his purview. Simplifying procedures became more important than troop morale. So there were no passes from this Replacement Depot situated on the edge of a city even though we had nothing better to do but wait for transportation back to Germany. Infractions, we were warned repeatedly, would result in cancellation of family allotments and other dire punishments. And no exception was made for an event so insignificant as the winning of the war. Generals do not serve in wars, they are served by them. War is the general's stepping-stone to the corporate directorship, the college presidency, and beyond.

A ship's whistle blasted jubilantly in the distance and set off a chain of responses across the harbor. My urge to bust free of the camp became more insistent. I wanted to be among these people who had suffered six years of war, who knew the agony of defeat and national humiliation; to share with them this end to pain and waiting now that the endless wait had ended.

It was then that Johnny DeWitt said, "Jesus Christ, men, we've got to celebrate tonight." And we were all agreed.

Just after dark Johnny, Doug, and I went over a low wall bordering the road into the city. A group of G.I.'s were lounging along the wall and one of them called out, "There they go, the officers are making a break." We didn't look back.

It was downhill all the way into the city and we stepped along eagerly, anxious not to miss any of the excitement. The semi-rural outskirts soon gave way to a bleak working class district and we stopped in front of a neighborhood bar to peer inside. There were only four or five customers sitting around engaged in restrained conversation. The area was quiet with no sign of festivity, so we continued on in search of the crowds we were expecting to find.

We finally arrived at the main business district still without coming upon any celebrants and all the people we encountered were seriously intent upon their own affairs. I looked into passing faces, reaching out for some sign of recognition, some mutual sharing of an inexpressible sense of having come through. Yet it was a feeling compounded by a deep melancholy whenever my mind's eye settled on the faces of the many friends and comrades who lay tonight in cemeteries along the route from Normandy to the Rhineland. Most of them had not known for what it was that they were fighting, and if they had lived they would not know what it was that they had won. But life alone would have been enough; that they understood with a zest that only the young have for living.

I felt a terrible need to make contact with just one person who could understand how this afternoon's news had excited my senses and exacerbated my soul. But the faces into which gazed only reflected the private concerns of harassed human beings. It was as if the spirit of celebration that had seized them earlier in the day had congealed in a special knowledge common to Frenchmen that although this war was over nothing much would be changed and there would be others. They were too long-enduring, too privy to the predilections of mankind, to share my naïve faith in this final triumph of common sense.

After a while we abandoned our quest and started back to camp disappointed and defeated, our plans for a big night evaporated in the indifferent air of Le Havre. Johnny and Doug chatted while I walked in silence contemplating the sky, and we were soon retracing our steps through the proletarian streets. As we were passing a vacant lot, a door opened on the far side and in the sudden beam of light we saw two U.S.

Marines in dress blues emerging unsteadily from the bar, their feet carefully testing the ground. There was an immediate revival of hope as we bore down on the light and slipped inside the door just as the portly proprietor brought down the corrugated metal shutters with a loudly reverberating clang.

It was a small and most unpromising oasis in which we found ourselves, bare and soiled with age, with a ten-foot bar, half a dozen tables along two walls, the elderly pair who ran the place, and a waitress with few visible charms. A small group of G.I.'s were congregating on one side of the room and we established ourselves on the other. There were no Frenchmen among the patrons and, more to the point, no Frenchwomen. Our situation was improved only to the extent that alcohol in some of its more virulent forms was now being dispensed.

"At least," said Johnny, "we can get good and drunk. That's better than nothing."

The waitress was not to be seen so Doug went to the bar and brought back three glasses of calvados, the powerful white fermentation that is the proud product of Normandy's farmers. They were soon on their second, and third, but I sipped mine slowly, just keeping them company. Milkshakes were more my style.

On his next trip to the bar, Johnny got into a conversation with one of the soldiers and came back brimming with information.

"There's a babe who takes the guys upstairs. They say she's a marvel. You don't even have to move. She does everything."

"She'd go great in an old man's home," I said.

"They've all been going up," he said. "How about it."

"Not me," I said. "It sounds like one of your fraternity house shags, and I'm not that fraternal. But you go ahead and enjoy yourself."

"I want to see what she looks like first," said Doug. "You go ahead and report back to your old buddy."

Johnny returned to the bar and I saw him speaking to the old man. When I looked again a couple of minutes later, he was gone. To the left of the bar there was a narrow doorway leading to a flight of stairs.

He was back in a few minutes, more subdued than before.

"Well, how was it?" asked Doug.

"Just like they said. The broad's got a movement that would make a Swiss watchmaker proud."

Doug's eyes lit up with anticipation. "What does she look like?"

"That's her there," replied Johnny, pointing over the bar. The waitress had just come through the doorway and was washing glasses.

Doug's eyebrows shot up and for some reason, my stomach sank.

"Her?" Doug's one word query was fraught with shock and disbelief. "You're pulling my leg, you bastard."

"No, I'm not," said Johnny. "She's the baby, all right, the Queen Bee who's the main attraction around here. She draws the boys from far and wide to her theater of operations upstairs."

I took another look. The woman was small, rather plain, and approaching middle-age. Her hair was straight and colorless, tied back in a bun. She wore a gingham dress and flat shoes. She did not seem to be wearing any make-up. No mademoiselle from Armentieres, she.

"Well, she certainly doesn't dress it up with a lot of frills," I said.

"She's got nothing to sell but the quality of her services," replied Johnny. "And they come highly recommended."

"By gosh," said Doug, "if it's good enough for you, it's good enough for me." He caught her eye and moments later followed her up the stairs.

I quickly downed my drink in an attempt to drown the acute depression I was experiencing over the way in which our night of celebration had degenerated into something desperate and unpleasant. I wished fervently that I were already back in Germany with my Ranger Battalion, among friends with whom I could share the victory as I had shared the stench of battle.

Doug and the woman came back. She was not one to linger at her work. She crossed over to our table and said something which I could not translate but understood perfectly. It was my turn and she smiled her readiness. I must have been the only American in the room who had not climbed the stairs with her and thereby represented the only obstacle standing between her and a perfect record.

I declined her extended favors with politeness and she expressed surprise, indicating that I was passing up an opportunity that might never come my way again. She had as much confidence in her product as General Motors has in its.

Suddenly from without there came a loud banging on the metal shutters and the G.I.'s all jumped to their feet and raced for the stairway. The old man was yelling and gesturing for us to get moving.

"What the hell's going on?" I called out. And one of the soldiers shouted back, "It's the M.P.'s. This joint's off-limits."

We followed them through the doorway and into the darkness beyond as the old man slowly proceeded to give access to the Military Police.

I went up one flight of stairs, and then another, and then one more, and then I seemed to be alone. The others had all disappeared down corridors and into places of refuge I did not know. I had not gone this route before and above the bar the building was in total darkness. I stopped and listened to the murmur of voices from below. All else was deathly quiet. I leaned against the wall of the narrow corridor and tested the creaky floor beneath my feet. Then I remembered that I had left my overseas cap lying on the table in the bar. I felt like such a ridiculous fool. I could hear my future children asking,

"Daddy, what were you doing the day the war ended?" And I would say to them, "I was hiding from the M.P.'s in a French whorehouse, children, worrying because I had been so stupid as to forget my cap in the saloon downstairs." It was all too much to be borne.

Then I felt a soft hand on my chest, and a warm body pressed against mine. Circe had come and I, without the protection of the magic herb, was about to be turned into a donkey. How had she stalked me in the dark corridors when I could not even make out her features, which was just as well. She moved against me with precision and I knew that I was being handled by an artiste, a French Florence Nightingale come to minister to my pain.

"Pour le victoire," she whispered in my ear. And I thought, why not? To make contact with one human being, that's what I had wanted. And this was surely the best offer I would get tonight. She was France: shabby, war-ravaged, badly used, and importuning. And I loved France. "Pour le victoire," indeed.

She took my hand and led the way up still more narrow, twisting stairways until I made a mental note to take a good look at the building later from the outside. It seemed as if we had climbed five flights before she opened a door in what must have been the attic and pulled me inside. I stood in the center of a tiny room, unable to distinguish anything but the outline of a single bed along the wall. A light cord brushed against my hair and I reached out for it but she stayed my hand. Then she unhooked my belt, raised her skirt and lay down on the bed, waiting. I hesitated and then began to remove my pants.

"No, leave on," she said, and reached out to pull me toward the bed. A minute later she whispered, "No, lie still. Me do." And she did. It was fast. It was explosive. And it was nothing. An act of supplication on the altar of lust. A solo movement performed by a virtuoso.

Doug and Johnny were waiting for me in the bar. Everyone

else was gone. We laughed when they told me how Madame Proprietor had tossed her bar rag over my cap just as the M. P.'s were coming through the door. I think it was the only laugh we had all night.

We walked ... to the camp in silence, our footsteps falling softly on the paved roadway, our spirits muted by the futility of the night's events. It was D-Day plus eleven months and the war against Hitler was over. No graves would mark this unmined road, no snipers lurked in the fields. No artillery fire grew louder in the distance to chill the marrow of our bones. At the end of the road there was no bloody, godforsaken beach resounding with the cries of mortal agony. There was only a dreary Replacement Depot into which we would have to sneak undetected on the first leg of the long journey home.

"They (American G.I.'s) are very different now. Don't let anybody tell you they aren't. They need a lot of people speaking for them and telling about them—not speaking for fancy bonuses and extra privileges. You can't pay in money for what they have done. They need people telling about them so that they will be taken back into their civilian lives and given a chance to be themselves again.   —Bill Mauldin
Up Front, 1945

"We marched at first gaily and finally with great weariness but always with a feeling that at last we were beginning the final series of marches that would lead us home again—home, the one really profound goal that obsesses every one of the Americans marching on foreign shores."
—Ernie Pyle
Here is Your War, 1945

Chapter Sixteen

Post War

There has been something misplaced in your son,
cause I cannot bring myself to write regularly.
—Ace Parker

AFTER THE WAR part of the Allied forces' job was military government. As combat troops took over an area, personnel moved in to see to the administration of it. Our job was to get it all back running again so the civilian population would be taken care of, like city water and sewer. Shake all that out. This was in Germany. France would take care of their own.

A city had the right to declare itself "open" which meant that it would not show any resistance. Germany was falling so fast that they ran out of Military Government Personnel. So they grabbed whoever was up there. Our Battalion Headquarters group and two companies of the 5th Rangers set themselves down in Weimar—the capitol city. That region included Weimar, Apolda, and Yena. I had Apolda, a city of about 35,000 people.

The first thing I did was get some interpreters in there. I ran things from the mayor's office in the Rathaus or city hall. I found a couple to be my interpreters who had come out from Berlin to escape the bombing there. In Berlin, the couple had run a tourist bureau in normal times. They spoke perfect English.

This couple told me that when Hitler first got hold of the government, he was really a hero of the people. He would send his men out and they would come into their homes and take a look around. They would say, "Gee, that's an awfully old refrigerator. You need some new equipment here." Then they would write out an order form and give it to them. Hitler had the whole populace behind him. But then the "brown shirts" started the atrocities. They got rougher and rougher the more they got into power. Finally, the thinking Germans could see what was happening and the trouble they were in.

Another individual I remember was Mr. Mall. He was a gentleman who had a small factory of some kind. He had seen what was coming prior to the war and had moved part of his manufacturing to England. He only got part of it moved before the Nazis stopped him from moving any more. As a punishment for his actions, the local political Nazis in the town mounted an air raid siren right on his apartment building. So, when it went off, it was just unlivable. He was also prevented from buying anything—clothes and such. The Nazis were known for doing just little humiliating things like that. When the American troops came in to help govern the town, the German residents of Apolda wanted somebody to represent them. They went to Mr. Mall because he spoke perfect English. They wanted him to come along and meet the officers of the unit that were taking over the town. They wanted him to talk with them and try to hash things out so that their town would be declared open and wouldn't be bombed or hit with artillery. And he told them, "I can't represent the town dressed as I am in these old clothes and my shoes are all worn out." So they outfitted him with a brand new suit and new shoes. Then Mr. Mall came and met the troops.

A town of 35,000 in Europe is a good drinking town. They had maybe half a dozen liquor warehouses. The refugees and slave labor people knew where every one of them were located. The city leaders wanted to prevent people from breaking in, getting drunk and going off on rampages and killing citizens. So we printed up signs in 4 or 5 different languages. We tacked these up on the warehouses to say that the Americans had been there and that all the liquor was sealed and removed from there.

Another duty of ours was to award passes. Of course doctors needed passes to allow them to be out on the street at night. They also needed a car and gas. We took care of this.

Apolda was a nice town. It also had two labor camps. Polish and French prisoners were put in the camps. The camps were allowed to organize their own internal affairs. They placed guards on the prisoners, confined them behind wire and used them as labor to repair the streets and buildings. They had all this manpower and they used it. I don't imagine that it took many soldiers to guard them.

Then a local group came to me, some representatives of a manufacturing firm. They wanted to know if I would have dinner with the manufacturing managers and several of the board members. I said sure. I took my runner and told him to keep an eye on things. I put on what Class A's (army dress uniform) that I had. When I arrived, they were all in evening dress, with black tie and boiled shirt. The dinner was held in the boardroom, right in the factory itself. They spoke English well. This was their dilemma. Germany was divided up post war between America, England, France and Russia. Berlin itself was divided up between those same nations. The Allied governments, Churchill, Stalin, and Roosevelt, determined how it was to be divided. What they wanted to get out of me was an idea of who was going to take over the area when we left, because the Russians were not far away. If it was going to be the Americans that took over and became the occupation government, then things could be pretty decent. However, if this area was going to slide over to Russia, then they were in trouble. Everything in that plant would be shipped over to Russia. They would be brutalized individually. Russia would come right into the houses and strip everything they owned that was decent, refrigerators and stoves, and send it back by the trainload to Russia. Understandably, they didn't want to be placed in the Russian zone. Russia may have been our Ally, but they were never our friends.

For my efforts in just listening and for whatever influence I might be able to generate, the representatives gave me a Contraflex camera. The entire top of that camera was the lens that you looked into. That was maybe about 3 by 3 inches. The shutter speed on it was 1/1000. I could take a picture with it and stop a softball right in mid flight without it being blurred. But I could not tell them what was to be their future.

Then there was the citizen's hour at which time the residents of the town could come by and make a complaint. One of them set me back blustering a little. An old woman came up to the desk; it was now her turn. As occupying troops, we had taken over the local houses for the troops to stay. That was acceptable. We weren't housed in barracks, but instead, all of us were in housing. This woman was complaining that the Americans had taken over her house and that the soldiers there were making a play house out of it with women over and such like that, which hurt her sensibilities. "Well, we will certainly take care of that," I reassured her. "Where is your house?" She gave the address. It was my house!

Later we were employed as a peace-keeping police force in Bavaria outside Munich, in the Alps with the high mountain lakes and chalets! The Nazis would come down into the villages and spend the night and then slip back out and go up into their mountain hiding places. We would make raids on the little villages by infiltrating during the night and then just as dawn would come, we'd catch them going back up. We could pick up wanted Nazis this way. They were in their worn out uniforms, having just been discharged. Many of them were wounded. We just took whoever we caught and turned them over to the MPs. Then they would sift them out as to who they were and who was wanted.

We also became a police or patrol section for the 12th Army Corps Artillery. The Americans and the French were manning the border crossings. I, for instance, became a liaison for a French officer. The two of us would check out the border guards wherever there was trouble. Nobody was shooting now. The war was over. The Americans were occupying Bavaria and the French were occupying Austria. We would be in camps along the road, set up in tents. There was a lot of trouble between the American troops and the French troops manning the check points at the borders. The French had very little, if anything, that wasn't given to them by us. The French border guards in Austria wore our uniforms and used our guns and equipment, which was a sore point. To make matters worse, our GIs would tease them about it. And so, there were always clashes.

The French, of course, had no sympathy and no pity for the Germans. The French soldiers on guard at the entry into Austria from Bavaria, would shake down every German convoy that went through there—not the military ones but the civilian ones, and take anything they wanted. The Germans couldn't do a thing about it. But then the Germans would complain to the military government. The French Lt. and I would drive out there. We would lecture and investigate. "You've gotta quit doing that fellas." We would observe for a while and then move on.

The Germans were moving across the border all the time, everything they owned piled high on trucks. This French Lt. had a civilian car, a nice big powerful two-seater. This crazy French Lt. would drive through this one town in particular, at 60 miles an hour. Eventually, they would shoot at us. There was nothing I could do about stopping him. Until finally, one day I told him that I would not ride with him anymore. That would reduce his authority at the checkpoints.

We heard that a German cavalry unit that had been in

France, 700-800 horses with all the tack and saddles, was breaking up. We could take some horses as long as we called it a school. So I established a riding school! Half a dozen of us went down to the cavalry where they were being discharged. We picked out some 30 horses and brought them home.

We rode the horses back to headquarters, some 35-40 kilometers (close to 20 miles). As I rode up, still on the horse, I told Sullivan, "Sully, this is the damnedest, easiest gait horse I've ever been on." He said, "Ace, get off that horse." He took her. Then it was Sullivan's horse.

At this time some of the guys became friends with a German girl, some kind of baroness or something. She rode beautifully as did all the German nobility. One day, she was on one of the horses. We were in a town with streets that were made of bricks. Of course, they were hard and shiny after centuries of foot wear, tire wear and everything else. Her horse started to run away with her. I was on a horse beside her. I managed to get ahead and grab the bridle of her horse and stopped him before the horse went down. He would have thrown her. Another memory for me. Some of the guys that went back and forth to Europe after the war made contact with her and her family.

Those days I remember as real relaxed living. Army script was an official IOU which could be redeemed and used to acquire civilian items so that we weren't just confiscating them. It was a legitimate transaction. I used army script to pay for the barley and oats to feed the horses.

Same thing with cameras. We also acquired good cameras for all the guys. We were to take all the German cameras from the homes as cameras could be used to take pictures of troop movements. This would be an intelligence that the Americans didn't want them to have. We had a guy, an apprentice camera man, from Hollywood. So this apprentice was told, "Pick out a camera with a good lens for every man in the company." We took a pack of cards. We put a card face up on each camera. Then we took another pack of cards and had each man draw a card. If he drew the ace of diamonds, for instance, then he went to the camera with the ace of diamonds. "Here, that camera is yours." So everybody got a good camera. I think I still have my 127. I don't think that they make 127 film anymore, however. It had a real fast shutter on it and a good lens.

We also confiscated all weapons that might be capable of injury. Ceremonial knives, sabers, everything. So, all of these things were piled up down in the city hall area or the plaza. And guns. Oh, the guns! Silver inlays of hunting dogs and such scenes would be on the breeches. These guns were just piled up in the middle of the town square. We poured gasoline and oil on them and then burned them. That could make a fella cry, as many of those guns might be worth thousands of dollars individually.

After the war was over we got a chance to relax and tour. It was sure good duty. Just the playground of the area. Jack Snyder and George Miller and I were kind of a trio. George was the best friend that I ever had. He was absolutely unflappable and absolutely "panic-insured against"! He had a great sense of humor and a silent laugh. If one of us had any money, play money that we didn't send home, we all went out.

We went up into the Bavarian Mountains and saw some castles. There were beautiful chalets up there. These had been built during the German glory years. In one place, there was a big resort that Hitler sent the SS people and the typical beautiful, acceptable German woman, to breed the ultimate German man. The Nazis also attempted to wipe out cripples and anybody with a genetic fault. The resort was a reward for these SS people. They could play away from all danger. They loved Hitler.

Hitler had a hideout constructed on the top of a mountain

peak called the Eagle's Nest. They had built a good tar road up to it, curved with sides reinforced and valleys that dropped away from it. The road led up to double, massive brass doors. After entering those doors, an elevator took you up to the Eagle's Nest. At the base of the hideout there was a poured concrete building—the SS barracks. A guard was stationed down below. Before anyone could reach those brass doors they had to fight their way through the SS guards. The window in that thing looks over a deep, deep valley all the way across. I have a picture of me in that window and I am as a speck standing in the window. It was massive. Hitler's hideout was heavily bombed by the Allies. This was in the Berchtesgaden area.

May 28, 1945

Dearest Mother and Dad, Carmen and all,
I'm in Reid, Austria doing nothing and thoroughly enjoying it. We're processing the German PWs but that's nothing.
It's been a long time since I've written. There has been something misplaced in your son, cause I cannot bring myself to write regularly.
Yesterday, I and Capt. George Miller took a jeep and rode up in the Alps Mountains. We went to Berchetsgarden to Hitler's house. It of course has been bombed and is in ruins, but nothing could destroy the beauty of the country. It is probably the most heavenly, beautiful spot in the world. All around are the Alp Mountains, with their peaks and sides covered with snow. We stood in snow up to our hips and threw snow balls at each other. Of course, we took millions of pictures. One of the best subjects, I think, was an old man straight as an arrow and seamy faced, who was dressed up in his Sunday best Bavarian alpine costume. You see many others like him here in

this country. Young and old dressed in short
leather pants with a halter like suspenders
all done in fancy many colored stitching. The
Alpine hat has a tassel of feathers and is
very pretty and picturesque.

The road was made by hand up the terrific
slope as many places had to be tunneled
through parts of the hill. The end of the
road stops at the elevator, which takes you
up to the "Eagle's Nest". Once there, you
have reached the highest peak and can look
down on the rest of the Alps around you.
There is one peak higher, but it's just an
insurmountable slab of stone not far from
"Eagle's Nest". Far down below is the lake as
blue as a sapphire and just as sparkling,
it's icy-cold and clear-fed from the snows on
the peaks. The whole country there in the
Alps, is something one can never forget.

The last time I was in combat I strictly
got religion. I prayed while crouching,
walking, rushing, running and while shooting.
Things were rough for a while.

This experience shook me up even though I
was able to stay in control of everything
going on, including me. I feel sure I'll be
home for Christmas. That is only a guess but
it's a good one, beyond that I have no idea
what the future in the army holds for me. I
can hope, but one never knows. God bless you
all, all my love. Charles.

Louis Gombosi met a Russian girl after the war was over.
We were in Markt Graffing, a town about 35 kilometers
southwest of Munich. The Russians put out an order working
through Roosevelt. Our government agreed to help pick up
Russian refugees and put them in boxcars and ship them back
to Russia. By this time Gombosi was really in tight with this
girl. She was an educated person. Well, we very, very
reluctantly complied until we found out that anybody

"contaminated" by democratic influences outside of Russia, which included students, were being shot when they got back to Russia. That stopped our compliance with the order. Three Russian officers had contacted this girl and told her that she had to go back. So she told Gombosi. Gombosi knew how to handle himself now. And Gombosi told Rooney. Sergeant James Rooney! Sergeant Rooney was a force to behold. A black-haired Irishman. A huge man…and built into that hugeness was just one of those animal muscle systems, a keen response system.

Gombosi and Rooney formed a group when they found out that the Russian officers were coming after her. He and Rooney met them. The Russian men were pretty darn husky too because they expected resistance. It was an epic fight. And of course Gombosi and Rooney won. Gombosi went into Munich and introduced the girl to the Red Cross. He said he wanted the Red Cross to give her a job and he wanted to know about it right now. He said he couldn't take her back. He had to go back by Army transportation under orders. But the minute his feet hit the American shore and he could effect discharge he would be back over and pick her up. He said he wanted to find her still working for the Red Cross. It turned out that way. They later married.

Next to Rheims, just outside of Paris, was a tent city that had the capacity for 55,000 troops. We went there on the way out of Europe. I was allergic to the tents and developed a massive case of urticaria or hives. As a matter of fact they had to give me a shot of adrenaline to knock it down. So I spent a lot of time out of the camp in Paris, which was not a bad deal! I financed it by the sale of the camera (the camera received from the Germans in Apolda) to a camera shop in Rheims. It was much more camera than I could utilize. My picture- taking was to snap a few photos every now and then. I got 1,200 U.S. dollars for it, which I pretty much blew in

Paris. We would go into Paris for three or four days at a time. I had a hell of a good time! Oh boy, we did the whole city! The prices at that time were piddly compared to what they are now. I think I stayed at the Metropol. I went in many times as it wasn't very far from Rheims. Our top officers had all gone home. This made George Miller and I in charge of the battalion. George, being a captain longer than I, had me on seniority. So he was the acting commander and I was the executive officer. We took turns traveling, but mostly into Paris. We'd just get a jeep and travel around. I would take a jeep generally by myself, sometimes with somebody else. I would take the distributor out of the jeep at night and chain the steering to whatever was available, a light post or something, in front of the hotel where I stayed. This was done so that nobody, GIs mostly, could steal it.

The atomic bomb had been dropped on Japan and ended the Pacific campaign, so we were no longer needed to go over there. The war was now over on all fronts. We went home together as a unit.

"The love of my life –Lois."

Jeff
Victoria   Laura
Kathryn

Epilogue

AFTER THE WAR Ace came home to every day life in the good old United States of America. He married Lois Gysler on April 12, 1946 and together they had four children, Jeff, Victoria, Laura and Kathryn. Getting up and going to work each day was a part of the package. Charles became a regional sales representative for Pfizer Pharmaceutical Company. He retired after 28 years with the organization.

In the darkness of the night he would yell out, wrestling with imaginary foes. His wife, frightened at his fierceness, would awaken him with a broomstick propped in the corner. It was kept there in the bedroom for just that purpose. For a long time he would wake up and be on his feet all in the same instant. His family could only guess that whatever he had lived through in the war must have been terrifying. He kept quiet for the most part about the war since Charles was not inclined to telling tales. The cartoonist Mauldin puts into words the difficulty encountered by returning war veterans to civilian life in which the civilians around them had no understanding about what war was really like:

> Often soldiers that are going home say they are going to tell the people how fortunate we were to stop the enemy before he was able to come and tear up our country. They are also going to tell the people that it is a pretty rough life over here. I've tried to do that in my drawings and I know that many thousands of guys who have gone back have tried to do it, too. But no

matter how much we try we can never give the folks
at home any idea of what war really is. I guess you
have to go through it to understand its horror. You can't
understand it by reading magazines or newspapers or
by looking at pictures or going to newsreels. You have
to smell it and feel it all around you until you can't
imagine what it used to be like when you walked on a
sidewalk or tossed clubs up into horse chestnut trees
or fished for perch or when you did anything at all
without a pack, a rifle, and a bunch of grenades.[7]

In 1959 or 1960, when Charles and his family were living
in a suburb of Chicago, one of the 1st Sergeants that had served
with him in the war came by pushing an ice cream cart
mounted in front of a bicycle. Charles walked out to get some
ice cream for the kids, who were still very young at the time,
and both men immediately recognized one another.

The two men had a long talk and Charles found out about
the reunions being held for Rangers from World War II. He
attended reunions in Chicago, Baltimore, San Diego and San
Antonio. Some of the Rangers never missed a single reunion.
Charles had already missed three or four by the time he found
out about them.

The reunions serve the purpose of bringing together men
that at one time kept each other alive, had been the family
away from home and had preserved each other's sanity
amongst the bombs, deaths and utter chaos. At one time these
men had meant a lot to each other. They still do. Wilbur
Ingalls probably captures the sentiment of these war veterans
most honestly:

> "When the men get together at Ranger reunions,
> then the stories start. People get a little shook up when
> I say this, but the feeling was, and I imagine that Ace
> feels the same way, we felt closer to those men than
> we did our own families. Actually, I'll say this, that
> there's never a day in my life since, that I haven't

thought of those guys. Sometime during the day they'll come to mind. We were just children, young men—20 years old, 21 or 22. We were at a time in our lives when everything had been quiet. We came from quiet little towns. And then bang, our lives were completely changed. And we were with these guys for life and death. We depended on them for that. We were of an age that we thought we could do anything, we really believed it. If we had a mission to do, we believed we could do it, and we did it."

Newsletters circulate several times a year and keep the men informed of each other's lives, including announcing those who have passed on. Many of the veterans can no longer travel. Some of the chapters have already disbanded.

Celebrations have taken place in France to commemorate the Anniversaries of D-Day. At the 40th celebration Ronald Reagan spoke of the Rangers: "These are the men who took the cliffs. These are the Champions who helped free a continent. These are the Heroes who helped end a war."

Joe Drodwill recalls revisiting Omaha Beach, Normandy, France, on the 45th Anniversary:

"I stood on the beach in the same spot that I landed, about 125 yards from where we let off from the landing craft. I was alone and it was very peaceful. I closed my eyes and I could see men (or boys) falling all around me. I could hear machine guns from the bunkers blazing and I could see the sand around me bounce up and spray. I can see an LSD take a direct hit from an 88 shell and explode with men blown into the air like match sticks. I can see the beach covered with a haze of smoke from fires started by shells from our ships. I remember men (or boys) crying and some asking for help, others just moaning, but I couldn't stop to help. I can hear bullets hit their target. I could hear and see 88 shells exploding on the beach just where I was a minute ago. I didn't feel afraid, just bewildered.

"I remember making the sea wall and stopped for a fresh breath of air. I looked back out in the ocean and could see the armada of boats. Some firing and some just sitting there. I never saw so many boats in my life in one place. I remember looking up from the sea wall to see if I could spot any machine gun emplacements. I couldn't find them, but above the noise of the war I could hear them and still can hear the cries of our men (boys) dying. I remember how the hills above were in a haze of smoke. I tried to look for my men. I remember finding most of them. I can't seem to remember how long we were at the sea wall but I don't think that it was very long. All this seemed to stand still, nothing seemed real. I was in another world.

"I remember machine guns firing from bunkers on our right raking the beach with their fire. I also remember machine gun fire and small arms fire from the hills in front of us and from the hill above. I lost some of my men at the sea wall but I don't know how many. I remember two men from our company (Bender) blew the barb wire on the beach with a bangalore torpedo. We went through the wire and off the beach into a mine field. All this I remembered as I stood on Omaha Beach at Normandy. This I remember was the start of the longest day of my life."

Charles "Ace" Parker attended the 50th Anniversary in France along with his son Jeffrey and his nephew Gerald. Ace recounts:

"Revisiting the Omaha beach 50 years later on the anniversary, I picked up a couple of rocks from the shingle on the beach. Visiting that beach was hard, particularly so since one old rusty wrecked assault boat remained out there. They've never moved it. It was quite a ways out but particularly showed at low tide."

Gerald, Ace's nephew, remembers the expedition to France on the 50th Anniversary:

"We got to the Newark airport. We were ushered to an area where the Rangers were collecting for their flight. Finally, we could see a bunch of older gentlemen off in a room. All of a sudden Chuck took off. My first impressions were, these were 'the guys' and that a very important person (Chuck) had just shown up. Chuck just got lost in the crowd. You know, I've never been at a Ranger reunion. I've never seen any of these men. There was an intimacy there that was unbelievable to witness. To have shared those kinds of experiences! I started to realize how special these relationships were.

"Jeff and I, following around, were rapidly identified by who we were with. A lot of wives would come up to us and tell us things; their impression of how their husbands had talked, how it was and that they would have never made it without Ace and without his leadership.

"Being with these 80 some Rangers, going over with them and spending all the time in the buses and getting together with them at banquets and that sort of thing, I came to realize that the whole group had just an aura of greatness about them. At the Normandy Cemetery I also realized that there wasn't much difference between them (the veterans) and the guys underneath the ground, other than a little bit of luck or a few inches.

"The Rangers to the French, from my impressions, were like saints. Everywhere the Rangers went, they honored them. They were minting medals to give to these guys—every French town had made their own to present to them. They had ceremonies. The mayor would stand up and speak and the dignitaries of the villages would stand up and speak, because they were so damned happy to have these fellows back. The French people of that area, particularly, do really indeed have a great deal of feeling for the Rangers. In Grand Camp there is a Ranger Museum. It has been 50 years and it is still going. You hear that the people in France do not like Americans. That could very well be true, maybe the younger ones. But not true for these people.

"We (his family) need to feel very proud of Chuck. He was not just a part of this but led in the thing. I don't understand how that happens. Here's somebody from this little town. What is there in this little town that could ever contribute to a person to inspire him to do what Chuck did?"

Ace Parker achieved an honorable status when he was inducted into the Ranger Hall of Fame on August 20, 1998. Membership into the Hall of Fame is limited to those who have served in a Ranger unit in combat or have graduated from the U.S. Army Ranger School. Nominations are based on valor, service and extraordinary achievement.

With this award his family came to appreciate what he had done in the war. Questions were asked. The stories poured forth, never forgotten, even after more than 50 years. The following letter announces the award:

Office of the
Regimental Adjutant
Ranger Battalion Association of World War II

Dear President,
    It is with great honor that I write to
inform you that Charles H. Parker has been
selected as a member of the Ranger Hall of
Fame. With this selection, Charles H. Parker
joins a select group of Rangers, which
includes BG William O. Darby and MG Frank D.
Merrill. Through his dedication and devotion
to his fellow Rangers, he richly deserves to
be remembered with this select group in the
Ranger Hall of Fame.

Sincerely,
Andrew K. Schweikert
LTC, IN
Adjutant

It wasn't long before newspaper write-ups began appearing about the local hero. This letter came from an appreciative citizen in Iowa:

August 19, 1998

Dear Mr. Parker:
    This morning I read with interest an
article about you in the St. Paul Pioneer
Press newspaper. The article explained your
induction into the Ranger Hall of Fame. I
want to congratulate you and thank you for
the contribution you made during World War II
to maintain democracy and freedom for our
country.
    After seeing the movie "Saving Private
Ryan," all of the D-Day and World War II
history I learned in school many years ago
came rushing back to me. Now, as a husband
and father of two young children,
remembering those who fought and died for

the United States just seems like the right
thing to do.

Since I don't personally know a World War
II veteran, I was determined to find your
address after reading the newspaper article—
and send you a thank-you for your efforts
made more than 50 years ago.

Americans forget the importance of
freedom, patriotism, honor and respect for
our country. It's unfortunate that it takes a
Hollywood movie to remind us of the tragedy—
and importance—of the people who fought for
the United States.

Thank you, Mr. Parker, for your valiant
efforts as a member of A Company of the 5th
Ranger Battalion. You are a true American and
your contributions will not be forgotten.

Sincerely,
Chuck Grothaus
Sioux City, Iowa

Ace Parker, at the age of 79, proudly attended the ceremony
that officially inducted him into the Ranger Hall of Fame.
Wilbur Ingalls was also there. Wilbur, now residing in
Michigan, drove himself all the way to Ft. Benning, Georgia,
for Ace's induction into the Ranger Hall of Fame. "I was going
to be there no matter what!"

Parker was one of 10 men, four of whom are deceased,
inducted into the 75th Ranger Regiment Association's Ranger
Hall of Fame at Fort Benning's Ranger Memorial. Escorted by
a Ranger on each arm, he proudly walked to the podium. He
delivered his acceptance speech to family, friends and 1200
active duty Rangers. He had carefully contrived a speech to
say that day, but upon arriving at the podium, he threw caution
to the wind and spoke from the hip. With a twinkle in his eye
and a humbleness that told much about his character, he
charmed the crowd with these words:

"During these things you wonder what you're doing here. It is very hard on an occasion like this to think of what to say. I think that I will just thank, in particular, Mike Zifcak, who did all the paperwork. And my family. Our four children are here with me. My brother is here with two of his boys. I'm sure that this event, generation by generation, will be molded into the family history. I should mention that the condition of my back has nothing to do with the war. I had a crack there recently. I'm extremely grateful for the shoulder. (Here he smiled at the two young Rangers at his side.) I'm usually in a wheelchair, but I wanted to be on my feet when I got this. I thank everybody."

The simple speech was followed by a spontaneous standing ovation from the audience. Ace Parker was a hero on that day and all the days he served his country in World War II. He "led the way" for freedom, democracy and basic human rights, all the gifts that we enjoy today. May we never forget *all* the heroes of World War II and all the wars fought for these privileges. May we always remember. Veterans Day and Memorial Day are not just days for picnics and boating, hot dogs and ice cream sandwiches. These are days for heroes, all the men that have bravely fought for our country, to honor and remember the sacrifice that they made for us and to teach our children so that they may teach their children. Thank you, Uncle Chuck—Ranger Ace Parker.

"Ace" Chuck Parker

Just stop
and you'll
remember,
When he left
he was
just a boy
but he
fought for
peace
and safety,
and the
other things
you enjoy.

Fifty years later, visiting Omaha Beach for the first time after D-Day, with son, Jeff.

You Say We've Changed

By Joe Drodwill, 5th Ranger Battalion

Take a boy off the grocery wagon, Take the kid that lives next door,
Put him in two months of boot camp, Send him out to fight a war.
Put a rifle on his shoulder, And a bayonet in his hand,
Tell him he's now a RANGER, That he's got to be a man.

Teach him how to kill a man, cause that's the way wars are fought,
Tell him he's a darn sight tougher, Than the Tojo's got.
Teach him cussin, swearing, fighting, Tell him he's hard and tough,
That he is fighting for his country, And all that patriotic stuff.

Send him away from women, Where men are all he ever sees.
Make him eat out of greasy mess gear, Where there ain't a word such as
    please.
Make him live just like a RANGER, eating, sleeping, on the ground.
Teach him to be alert and wiry, And to notice every sound.

Let him see men when they are dying, From the battles that they have fought,
Let him hear their cries of terror, From the wounds that they've got,
Tell him a RANGER ain't sentimental, But will laugh at death and pain,
And that he's got to keep fighting, Cause he's got so much to gain.

Them that don't send him letters, Let him think that you've forgot,
About the one that's fighting for you, Where the sun is scorching hot,
Then let his girl start dating the draft dodger who lives next door,
And you've ruined all his spirit, Cause these are the things he's fighting for.

Bring him back home, And he'll be a little crude
Take him out on a little party, And he can't get in the mood,
And his manners won't be perfect, Like the guy who lives next door,
Who worked in the defense factory, While he fought in the war.

So you say we've changed, we're different, Not the kind of kids we were,
When we left you at the platform, And went off to fight this war.
But don't be too hard or too critical, When he makes mistakes galore.
Just be tolerant and keep smiling, Cause it's you he's fighting for.

Then why not let him have his fun, And other things he enjoys,
Go out dancing, whooping, drinking, With a few of the boys.
You say a RANGER has no heart, That he's not like other men,
That all he has in his heart is beer, whiskey, and gin.

But say! Just stop and you'll remember, When he left he was just a boy.
But he fought for peace and safety, And the other things you enjoy.
He has given all the best years, Of a life he has had,
Ask him why and he will tell you, He did it for his sweetheart, Mom and
   Dad.

Standing in pill box opening, Omaha Beach, 1994

Normandy Cemetary for the American soldiers just above Omaha Beach

ABOUT THE AUTHORS

Marcia Moen and Margo Heinen, identical twin nieces of Ace Parker, grew up on a farm in west central Minnesota. They visited their mother's brother, "Uncle Chuck," often and were good friends with his children—their "city cousins." Marcia graduated from Bethel College with a degree in nursing and is now a nurse practitioner residing in Elk River, Minnesota, with her husband. Margo Heinen graduated from the University of Minnesota with a degree in Education and now is a Sales Consultant living in Hudson, Ohio. They remain close inspite of the distance that separates them.

Charles "Ace" Parker, now 80 years old, resides in Anoka, Minnesota where he has lived for the last 39 years.

INDEX

REFERENCES

1. Haskew, Michael E. *World War II*, Feb. 1999, Editorial Page.
2. Army Historical Division. *Small Unit Actions*, Washington, D.C., April 4, 1946, p. 55.
3. Ibid., p. 55.
4. Ibid., p. 58.
5. Ibid, p. 58.
6. Ibid., p. 63.
7. Mauldin, William. *Up Front,* World Publishing Co., 1945, p. 128.

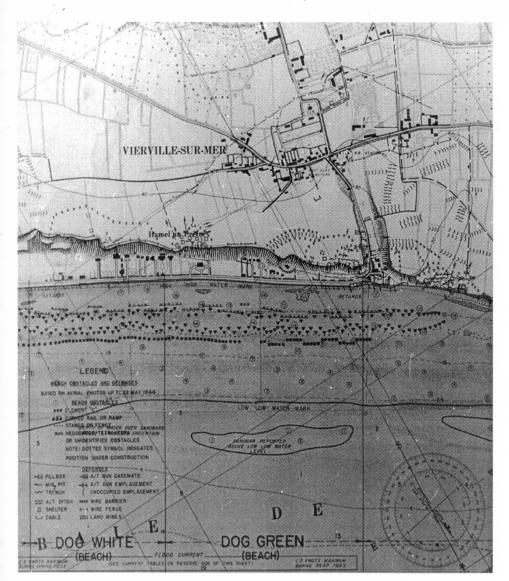

OMAHA BEACH-WEST (Vierville-sur-Mer)

"In the eleven months of combat, the 5th Ranger Battalion had fought its way from Normandy to Austria, killed an estimated 1,572 enemy and taken 4,541 prisoners. In doing so, it lost 155 killed, 552 wounded, 25 missing and 2 known captured."

from: Leavenworth Papers, Rangers: Selected Combat Operations in World War II, by Dr. Michael J. King